LATINAS RISING

BREAKING GENERATIONAL CHAINS & BECOMING CHANGE MAKERS

AMA PUBLISHING

Copyright © 2024 AMA Publishing

All Rights Reserved. Apart from any fair dealing for the purposes of research or private study, or criticism or review, as permitted under the Copyright, Designs and Patents Act 1988, this publication may only be reproduced, stored or transmitted, in any form or by any means, with the prior permission in writing of the copyright owner, or in the case of the reprographic reproduction in accordance with the terms of licensees issued by the Copyright Licensing Agency. Enquiries concerning reproduction outside those terms should be sent to the publisher.

CONTENTS

Foreword — 5

1. Criss Madrigal — 7
2. Darlene Menjivar — 20
3. Laura Tabarez — 34
4. Lizette Romo — 46
5. Maria Molina Monroy — 58
6. Marie Camacho — 70
7. Annett Velasquez — 84
8. Edilka Anderson & Carla Guzman — 95
9. Jasmine Murudumbay — 105
10. Jessica Coronado — 114
11. Liliana Bernal — 123
12. Dr. Marissa Vasquez — 133
13. Nikki Storms — 143
14. Patty Samudio — 154
15. YG Collaborations — 163

About AMA Publishing — 173

FOREWORD

I am beyond honored to introduce you to Latinas Rising: Breaking Generational Chains & Becoming Change Makers. This book is not just a collection of stories; it is a movement, a beacon of hope, and a testament to the resilience and power of Latina women.

My journey began in the most unlikely of places. Born into homelessness, I defied the odds to become a multi-millionaire by the age of 24 and achieved even greater financial milestones by 34. These accomplishments, however, are not the pinnacle of my story. My true purpose has always been to uplift and empower others, especially Latina women who face unique challenges and barriers.

Latinas Rising brings together the voices of incredible women who have shattered ceilings, defied stereotypes, and carved their paths to success. It is a collective narrative that speaks to our shared experiences, our struggles, and our triumphs. Each chapter is a reminder that we are not alone and that our dreams are valid and achievable.

As I reflect on my journey, I realize that the key to breaking generational chains is education, empowerment, and community. Through my work with The Latina Empire, I have committed myself to providing resources, mentorship, and opportunities to help Latinas recognize their worth, develop their skills, and achieve financial independence. Our mission is to impact the lives of 10 million Latinas by fostering a culture of peace, love, empowerment, and abundance.

The stories within this book align perfectly with this mission. They highlight the importance of perseverance, the power of community, and the transformative impact of self-belief. These women are not just authors; they are warriors, trailblazers, and change-makers. Their experiences and insights will inspire you to push beyond your limits and pursue your dreams with unwavering determination.

I champion this endeavor because I believe in the boundless potential of Latina women. We are the heartbeat of our communities, the innovators of our industries, and the leaders of today. By sharing our stories, we reclaim our narratives and create a legacy of strength, resilience, and success for future generations.

To every woman reading this book, I want you to know that you are capable of achieving greatness. Your background, circumstances, or the obstacles you face do not define you. What defines you is your courage, your passion, and your vision for a better future. Embrace your journey, celebrate your uniqueness, and never stop believing in yourself.

Together, we rise. Together, we break chains. Together, we become the change-makers the world needs.

With love and empowerment,
Perla Tamez Casasnovas

1
CRISS MADRIGAL

LIVE YOUR DREAM

You don't have to do it alone. You never did. You might have believed that, but remember, not every thought deserves your attention.

Life is not meant to do alone. We are designed to have a tribe. A group, *que en las buenas o en las malas, te levante*. A community of like-minded people who support you in an instant because they are walking the same path beside you.

I craved connection with people who not only saw me but also understood me on a cultural level. People who were defying cultural norms, ready to rise and shatter generational chains. People willing to put themselves first and chase their dreams, terrified but hopeful. I yearned for a space where we could grow together as we journey through life. A place to rise, feel supported, connect, collaborate, and elevate. And so, I knew I had to emerge from the cave.

THE JOURNEY

Reflecting on my childhood, I cherish the incredible moments spent living in Mexico. My parents provided my siblings and me with one of the most beautiful cultural experiences imaginable. It was their dream to one day return and live in Mexico, so they raised us by immersing us in the culture, spending six months in the U.S. and six months in Mexico.

I vividly remember the joy and excitement as December approached, signaling it was time to pack up and head to a place I loved dearly. My mom would pack the suitcases, rolling our clothes tightly like burritos to make it all fit. She filled the ice chest with drinks, food, and snacks, while my dad prepared the camper on the pickup truck, creating a cozy space for us. That setup became our home for the next two and a half days.

In retrospect, when we talk about our trips, we recognize just how unsafe they were. Our journey took us from Northern California into Arizona, where we would stop to sleep, only to wake up at the crack of dawn and continue into Mexico, traveling through Chihuahua, Zacatecas, Aguascalientes, and finally to our main destination, Yahualica, Jalisco!

I remember those long days on the road. My sister loved to play *name that tune*, and we would hum songs for hours, trying to guess each one. We all wanted a chance to ride shotgun with our parents and listen to their stories as we drove. So, if we were lucky enough, we made sure to turn around and smile at the other two in the back. Only to discover the back was a bit more exciting than the front row.

I could immediately sense my parents' anxiety rising the moment we crossed into Mexico. I vividly remember the time we were randomly stopped by strangers who circled our truck, flashing their lights inside. I could hear my mother's prayers, and the fear in her voice. Yet, despite these moments, we returned year after year, determined to give us an incredible childhood.

When we finally arrived in Yahualica, I was filled with joy and excitement to see the family and friends who awaited us year after year. We had kept in touch through letters, and everyone eagerly anticipated our arrival.

The months and years spent in Mexico were, without a doubt,

the best of my childhood memories. It felt as though our parents felt safe enough to let us roam freely with our friends. Our elementary school was just half a block from home, and middle school was my first experience in a private Catholic school where classes ran from 2 pm to 7 pm, as I recall.

Our mornings were filled with chores, from sweeping the cobblestone streets to washing clothes by hand and mopping daily. These weren't the fondest memories, but they taught me to appreciate the amenities I had in the U.S.

As I grew older, I began to recognize certain aspects of our culture that I didn't agree with, particularly when it came to the education system. I had a strong desire to go to college, but I couldn't see that possibility in Mexico. We weren't a family of status, nor did we have connections within the system. Back then, it wasn't about your grades or exam scores, it was about who you knew.

At that point, I decided to stay in the U.S. to pursue a higher education. Life as I knew it came to an end, and I chose to remain in the U.S. to chase the American Dream.

THE AMERICAN DREAM

One day, I woke up and realized I wanted a different life than the one I saw around me. I remembered the freedom I felt in Mexico. The genuine connections and the different lifestyle. I loved it and longed to have it back, but I couldn't see a way to recapture that feeling.

In the U.S., I didn't feel connected. I didn't feel seen or heard, and even though it was my birthplace, I didn't fit in. To break the cycle, I knew I had to leave the small town of 1,800 people we lived in and go to college.

As a first-generation college student, I had to figure everything out on my own, and so I did and left for college. I remember the night before my parents drove me to the dorms at San Jose State University; I was filled with anxiety and suddenly didn't want to move.

Although I was the youngest of three, I was the first to move away for college.

My family helped move me into the dorms, and as they walked away, I felt scared. I could see the fear in my parents' faces and the tears in my mother's eyes. We were all trying to be brave, but now I was on my own, in a big city, navigating life as a young adult.

My mother's greatest dream was to get an education, but she had to drop out of school in the sixth grade to work and help provide for the household. She was determined to ensure her children would obtain the education she was denied.

Was I living out her dream instead of my own?

I followed the traditional path. I went to college, earned three degrees, bought a house, got married, started a family, landed a corporate job, stayed in it for 19 years, earned six figures, but I wasn't fulfilled.

How did I end up here? What happened? Why didn't I recognize myself?

The signs were all there; I just chose to ignore them.

I chose the traditional path, the American Dream. But that dream had turned into a living nightmare.

My parents sacrificed so much to give us the opportunities they never had, and for that, I am eternally grateful. Yet somehow, I realized I was reliving their story, just with financial and educational upgrades.

I carried the same fears, adopted the same scarcity mindset, and allowed my employer to control a large part of my life.

If breaking the cycle was all I ever wanted, how did I end up feeling so trapped?

I was reliving the very path I didn't want, the path I had tried to break away from. I had the education and compensation my parents only dreamed of, yet I wasn't happy.

I hadn't broken the cycle of *FREEDOM*. Someone else owned my time, and in the process, I had given away part of my joy.

A corporation controlled my freedom.

A corporation dictated how many days off I could spend with my family.

A corporation determined my worth through an annual review—if I even received one.

The worst part was, I had allowed it to happen!

I had spent my entire adult life working tirelessly to make someone else's dream come true, but what about mine?

Where had my dreams gone?

At what point did I silence my inner voice and decide it was no longer important?

I looked around and no longer recognized myself. I was simply existing, not truly living or loving life.

Somewhere along the way, I stopped believing in myself. The child who once had big dreams no longer existed. Those dreams had become a distant vision, and if I was going to break the cycle, I had to start believing in myself again!

THE AWAKENING

It was time to live life differently! The familiar path had left me feeling drained, and I was officially done with it.

I began to make courageous moves.

I began to invest in myself.

I began to rediscover who I was before life told me otherwise.

I began to change my programming.

I began to connect with my higher self and spiritual guides.

And I began to see clearly again.

The path I once believed was right had led me to shackles. So, I quietly began the inner work. I had to find my tribe—the coaches, mentors, and communities that would uplift me during my awakening process.

Not everyone was on my side, and not just anyone was allowed on my team. I had to find my people. Let me tell you, it's a lonely journey when you're just starting out, but I pushed through.

There were moments when I felt like I was living a double life. I had to hide my journey from my employer after being told I was spending too much time on personal development, which they claimed would take away time and energy from my work. This was yet another confirmation that they didn't care about my best interests or growth—only the company's.

I decided to be brave and asked for time off to obtain my coaching certification at UC Davis. When it was approved, I felt hopeful that the organization might finally see my vision. With seventeen years in Human Resources under my belt, I thought, just for a moment, that they recognized my value and believed in my vision. But I was wrong.

When I shared my vision, one executive told me, "You think too big. You need to think smaller." Another said, "You will never be able to do that in this department."

That was the moment I said, *ENOUGH, CRISS*!

Stop letting others shatter your vision. You were meant for more!

So, on March 29, 2024, after nineteen years with the same organization, I closed the chapter on my corporate life. I became a full-time entrepreneur, ready to conquer my wildest dreams and elevate those who choose to rise with me.

THE UNLEARNING

I never imagined how much I had to unlearn from my years in corporate. I spent the first few months shedding beliefs that no longer served me.

I had always been a high performer, consistently accomplishing more in the same amount of time as others. I frequently joined teams to improve processes and increase productivity, but in the end, it all felt like meaningless work. It was just "busy" work that never led to lasting change.

What I did adopt was the hustle and grind mentality. I believed I had to work exceptionally hard for endless hours to create the life I desired. But boy, was I wrong!

After leaving corporate, I had to force myself to let go of this belief.

I began to work smarter, not harder. I challenged myself to work fewer hours and enjoy life more. Let me tell you, this doesn't happen overnight. I still found myself believing I hadn't done enough. That was until my mentor brought me to a screeching halt.

She said to me, "Criss, you place conditions on your happiness."

The comment hit me, and it hit me hard!

Was I unconsciously preventing myself from experiencing joy until certain tasks were completed each day?

Was part of my self-worth tied to how long I worked?

It hit me again!

I was STILL unlearning the lessons the corporate world had ingrained in me. It taught me that no matter how efficient I was, I still had to be present in the office.

I had been an unconscious competent my entire life, conditioned to create work just to fill my days in the corporate world. Over nineteen years, this added up to a significant amount of time. Efficiency was never rewarded. How dare anyone be so efficient and leave the office before others? Who do you think you are?

It took nineteen years to condition myself to a belief that left me depleted at the end of each day, and I no longer wanted that feeling. That programming began creeping in again as an entrepreneur, only this time, I was in front of a computer at home, and some days I felt my energy bank low by the end of the day.

That was until I realized that part of my purpose on this earth is to show others a new way.

A way that allows you to enjoy the beauty of this life.

A way that frees you from being enslaved to old beliefs, allowing you to adopt a new way of being.

A way that makes life and work feel effortless and joyful.

A way where happiness is unconditional, fully experienced with every fiber of your being.

That is what I am here to do—To show you a new way of life!

THE ELEVATION

Elevation comes with awakening your consciousness. It stems from believing in your capacity to receive messages from God, Source, the Universe, guides, or whoever you connect with. They are always speaking to you. The real question is, do you get quiet enough to hear them?

I began to close my eyes and truly feel God's presence with me. He had always been there, but my mind was too cluttered to hear His voice as clearly as I do now. Now, His words flow through me, and His messages are so profound that I capture them in a notebook to remember them.

I vividly recall the first time I heard His voice loud and clear. I closed my eyes, and His message flowed through me. With tears streaming down my face, I feverishly wrote down every single word that came through. I had never felt God so close. I had always prayed and believed deeply, but this time, it was DIFFERENT!

His message was so profound that it left me speechless. After breakfast, I sat at the kitchen table and told my husband about my experience. I couldn't find the words to describe it, so I grabbed my notebook and read the message aloud. It brought him to tears, and all he said was to obey.

These messages now wake me up in the middle of the night. They are so beautiful that I began capturing them on my phone to remember in the morning. One night, I woke up to the words, "Life is to learn and grow." I tuned in, then heard:

Life is to learn and grow.

Learn to love life from within, for it all starts in your heart.

Learn to embrace every moment with a smile even when it hurts inside, for a smile signals a feeling of love.

Learn that life is what you make it to be, not what you think it should be.

Learn to smile while exhausted, let it propel you in the right direction and not drown you.

Learning is part of your journey on earth to...

Grow in faith as you mourn.

Grow in love as you drown.

Grow in joy as you embrace life.

Most of all, grow within, and expand your capacity to receive all that is already yours.

You are one with God.

You are one with the universe.

You are the one in control of your mind.

Decide how you want to experience life today. Imprint that in your heart and allow that to be your truth.

My elevation has brought me new levels of faith, greater levels of trust, and profound levels of love. I have attracted people into my life who have led me to experience life in ways I never imagined possible.

At the start of this chapter, I mentioned my desire for connection with people who not only saw me but understood me. People who were defying cultural norms, ready to rise and break generational chains. People who were prepared to put themselves first and pursue their dreams.

This is what The Elevation brought me, my people!

The best part is that this journey has not only elevated me but also my marriage and, in turn, my family. I also wanted a place to grow together as we journey through life. A place to rise and feel supported. A place to connect, collaborate, and elevate, and I have found that in my own home. All I needed was to come out of the cave, see the light, and experience life differently.

I believe every moment in life is here to teach me something, and it's up to me to decide what to do with each lesson.

I was told that this book, *Latinas Rising*, was here to teach me something, but it was up to me to discover what that was. So, I got quiet. I asked God faithfully, and His answer flowed right through.

It's here to teach you to be fearless. It brought you a safety net to allow you to step away from corporate. You wouldn't have done it otherwise. It's teaching you to have faith in the unknown. To believe in the unseen. As you meditate on this book and the unknown, it's elevating your consciousness.

It's teaching you courage. Being fearless is also courageous. This book came to free you from corporate for you to share your experience in it. To launch a new company and see all the beautiful pieces come together.

It brought a mentor into your life to wake you up and show you how to do things easily. You've worked so hard up to this point. Allow it to be easy. I'm taking care of you. I'm taking care of your family.

It immediately became clear to me. *Latinas Rising* enabled me to ascend to new levels. To move through discomfort, release fears, and embrace my dreams. To expand and acknowledge my capacity to serve globally. To amplify the voices of women from diverse backgrounds. And to serve as a conduit for others' elevation.

THE TRANSITION

I am eternally grateful for this book and the transition out of the cave. While metaphorically speaking, it has truly brought immense light, so much love, and greater levels of expansion into my life.

Latinas Rising is the book that taught me how to navigate the unknown, to fully believe in my vision, and to trust wholeheartedly that things will unfold not as I plan, but as they are destined.

I am one with God.

I am one with the universe.

I create what I desire, but it starts with belief.

I must believe in myself, believe in my vision, and believe in my ability to create everything God has placed in my heart.

Every step forward brings me closer to my vision.

Every step forward opens a new path.

Every path is an opportunity for me to grow and expand.

This summer, Archangel Michael delivered a specific message to me. The first word that came through was *MAGIC!* He asked me, *where is the everyday magic in your life?* He wanted to remind me that I am always protected and cared for. Knowing this, he questioned how I could incorporate more magic and play into my life. He sensed that I sometimes shield myself from fully enjoying life. So, he challenged me to invite magic in and trust in the joy of his constant supportive presence.

And so, I loosened my grip and began to watch the magic unfold!

I don't know what my next chapter in life will look like. I don't know where my next client or work will come from. But I do know that the moment I began to loosen my grip, the moment I started to relax, the moment I began to have fun without caring what people would say, that was the moment I truly began to experience freedom!

I was told, if you want to predict your day-to-day, go back to corporate. But if you're seeking an expansive life, entrepreneurship is where you should be.

There's one thing I can certainly say, I have never felt more freedom, love, joy, and excitement for life than I do now!

God is my safety net; I will never truly fail. For each failure reveals to me what's on the other side, and I use every failure to propel me forward in life. Every failure serves as a redirection from my guides, leading me to places I would otherwise not discover.

I am here to make a significant impact on the lives of those I serve.

I am here to teach my children to dream big.

I am here to live my most abundant life.

And I am here to share it all with you!

For now, I invite you to follow me on all social media platforms and watch this beautiful journey unfold.

Let's connect! Tell me if you're ready to live out *YOUR* dreams!

To my husband, Americo: There is no doubt that I am meant to experience the wholeness of this world with you. Thank you for awakening the Goddess within me! I love you, and I hope you're ready for our next quantum leap in life and love!

To my mentor, Monique: I was unexpectedly guided to you, and I am so grateful I stayed for the journey. It has been one of the most enriching learning experiences filled with guaranteed laughter and fun! Thank you for being unapologetically vibrant in living life and for reminding me of who I am.

ABOUT CRISS MADRIGAL

Criss Madrigal is a first-generation Mexican American, the youngest daughter of immigrant parents, and a natural storyteller. Transitioning from a Fortune 500 leader to a mindset and growth coach, she has become an international bestselling author, speaker, podcast host, and publisher.

Live YOUR Dream is an intimate story of living the American Dream, until Criss woke up one day and realized she was living her parents' dream and not her own. This realization propelled Criss to leave her nineteen-year career in Human Resources to become a full-time entrepreneur.

Criss is now on a mission to elevate the voices of one million women worldwide by 2029 through her coaching, speaking, publishing, and podcasting endeavors.

Criss empowers and coaches highly successful women to embrace the power of their stories, guiding them to become bestselling authors and create lasting legacies.

Her goal is to inspire women to trust in their inner power and become influential changemakers within their own communities.

Website: www.crissmadrigal.com
Facebook: www.facebook.com/crissmadrigal.us
LinkedIn: www.linkedin.com/in/criss-madrigal
Instagram: www.instagram.com/crissmadrigal

2
DARLENE MENJIVAR

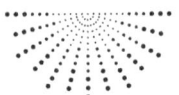

My mother was born in Guadalajara Mexico into a family of nine, with her 7 siblings and her single mother, my grandma "Concha." There are many family accounts that tell of how they all survived and the things all the children did, to bring home money, or food.

From robbing corn from nearby crops and avoiding the guard dogs; to the young boys bringing home a cow and enjoying free milk for a day, before the police came and took the branded cow back to its owner. My mother remembers knocking on doors and offering to wash people's dishes for a small fee. There was even a time when they were all homeless. However, what is most prevalent in these stories, are the laughs and the love between them all. How my grandma was able to handle these struggles, as a single mother, while maintaining laughter and love as the emphasized experience to 8 children, is truly incredible.

However, at 14 years old, my mother crossed the border with her 12-year-old nephew. They crossed with a "coyote," paid by one of her older sisters who needed her to come to babysit her children. My mother remembers it, as a nerve-wracking journey, and one where she held to dear life, a guardian angel my grandma had given her before she left. My mother mainly recalls the fear, and the prayers to that guardian angel, all the way to Chicago. She babysat for over a year before the children were able to go to school. Then another sister, this time in California, needed her to babysit. It took a 3-day drive from Chicago to Los Angeles, which she did scared, tired, and crying. Once those nieces and nephews grew up my mother was determined to not go through another trip. She gathered her older sister and brother who had recently crossed the border and rented an apartment together.

With this stable home, and my mother finding work, she flourished! She explored the city, worked in retail, and took hold of her life; free to live it on her own terms. She was a social butterfly and made friends easily. She was always attending Quinceañeras and weddings because she made it a side hustle to choreograph everyone's waltz dances. She lived and enjoyed her youth, her friends, and the LA city life. She was, and still is, a loving, confident woman who loves dresses and shoes. She was street smart, assertive, resourceful, and had dreams of opening her own hair salon. I am convinced, that if she had stuck with that dream, she would have a thriving salon business now. To start opening more doors for herself, she started taking English classes at night, where she met my father.

I'm the daughter of a strong, free-spirited woman, who doesn't follow anyone's rules. She has always encouraged me to live adventurously, to try new things, and to unapologetically choose myself. I am a daughter to a woman who takes no shit, and whose inner strength always shows. She's taught me to demand respect and stand up for myself. She's encouraged me to fight for what I believe in and speak up for others. She's filled me with love and empathy for our culture and people, and always reminds me where I come from. Because of her own family separation, she's made it a priority to keep her family together and feeling loved. She's shown me how to be a mother who showers her kids with love and affirmations and to never hold grudges, no matter what family conflicts come up. My mother is my spiritual sanctuary. She's the one that holds up my spirit when I am depleted from the world. She places belief in me when I can't find my own, and her words never fail to empower me. She is my loving football coach, who pushes me to be better. She is the one who sacrificed her dream for her children knowing that we will be her legacy. She is my example of raw self-love and relentless drive to just go for it.

My father was born in La Libertad, El Salvador, and grew up in San Juan Talpa. His mother, left him with his grandparents when he was young to find a better life in the U.S. My father's life was a bit more stable; he had a home and always had food, whether it was meals from his grandmother or fruit from the trees surrounding the house. However, his home was not as loving as my mother's. My father consistently experienced domestic abuse by my great-grandfather, "El Abuelo." El Abuelo used to be a tango professor and was a ladies' man. He worked and raised enough money to eventually purchase many acres of land, which were the acres my father grew up in. My father doesn't talk much about his childhood, saying he doesn't remember too much. But there are three stories that have been shared that shed some light on my father's childhood. He once mentioned my great-grandfather beating him with a yucca branch because he didn't harvest as many bags as my grandfather. My father was about 8 years old. Another time, he and my great-grandmother ran to the fields at night, because 'El Abuelo' had come home drunk and in a rage. My father still remembers the fear on my great-grandmother's face, praying they wouldn't be found. I heard another account, this time from his cousin; when as young boys, they were playing together and made a mess of some kind. When "El Abuelo" got home, his cousin quickly left for the safety of his own home, however, he could still hear my father's screams as my great-grandfather disciplined him from a few houses down.

My father was in El Salvador until he was 17 years old, when he made his first attempt to leave. Unfortunately, at the Guatemalan border, he was sent back. His second attempt was the successful one and ended up being the easiest. He made it to the U.S. by airplane, thanks to a family member who worked for immigration and was able to provide him with a visa. It must have been an amazing feeling to leave the abuse behind, especially in such a majestic machine. For someone with a poor memory, he clearly recalls, "It was a 747 airplane."

My father's only intention was to work. He started in a warehouse making plastic toys, then moved on to manufacturing aluminum parts, and eventually worked at the California LAX airport. Throughout these years, he was able to devote his attention to his passions and goals. My father loves to dance! He would go out to the disco club and dance until closing time. His movements earned him a reputation as a "great dancer," a title he is still called to this day. I'm convinced that if he had taken dance classes, he would have had a successful career in that industry. He was living life, making friends, and had a confident, silly personality. He set a goal to get a car and saved until he could buy a 1972 Chevy Camaro, blue with a white racing stripe, his most prized possession. He was looking to better himself and gain a better job, so he started taking English classes at night, where he met my mother.

I'm the daughter of a man who endured domestic abuse, and withstood years of beatings, yet it didn't break him. He taught me what it means to live authentically and to find silliness and joy in life, no matter the hardships that come your way. I am the daughter of a man who refused to continue the abuse he experienced, pouring love and wisdom into his children and showing me that cycles can be broken. I am the daughter of a man with a strong work ethic who taught me the importance of being detail oriented. This one skill alone has brought me much success in my own career. I am the daughter of a man who always worked labor jobs, sometimes in dangerous environments and for low pay, so that his daughter could focus on school, granting me the stability and space to gain several diplomas. My father instilled in me a love of music, exposing me to everything from cumbias, salsas, and trios to disco, rock, and pop, showing me the beauty and harmony of diversity. He sacrificed his potential to provide for our family, no matter the cost, and taught me the non-negotiable expectation of self-respect.

I would not be the person I am without my parents; they are the foundation of many of my values and passions. Their teachings and examples have guided me along my own journey. Both the positives and negatives of their experiences have shaped me into the woman I needed to be to face the journey ahead once I was no longer under their roof.

I was born in Hollywood, California. As a child, I enjoyed the beautiful weather, the city noises, and weekly visits to Echo Park with my mom. However, as amazing as California was, the tough economy made it difficult for my parents to achieve their biggest goal, buying a home. So, they left behind everything they knew... again. Family members from Mexico and El Salvador had settled in California, and my parents had built a network of family, friends, and a community throughout their young adult lives in the state. Yet, they knew that the city they lived in was not the ideal environment they wanted for me. They could see where I might end up if I continued in poorly funded schools with limited resources and few success stories beyond high school. They wanted something bigger for me and were eager to provide a great environment and home where I could thrive. So, when my mother's niece told her about the opportunities and affordable homes in Arizona, my parents went all in. I was 6 years old when, after a 6-hour road trip to Phoenix Arizona, we walked into a fixer-upper home with broken tile inside but with a wonderful little yard, my own room, and to my surprise, a pool in the backyard.

As we began our life in this new state, my mother did everything she could to prepare me for school. She bought me, what seemed to my little 6-year-old eyes, a gigantic chalkboard. She taught me how to write my full name, our house phone number, and our address. However, no matter how well I summarized this information, I was not prepared for what happened on my first day of school. I walked into class, where the teacher must have introduced me, but I immediately realized, I did not understand what she was saying. I did not understand a word of English! I was raised only speaking Spanish.

Once the teacher realized this, I could sense her disdain. My mother had to return to school to pick me up, where she was told her daughter did not speak English and, very coldly, was told she should look for another school with bilingual teachers. As we left, I told my mother in Spanish, "I don't care what it takes, I will learn how to speak English" " She saw the anger and hurt in my eyes and was taken back by the determination in my voice. We found a nearby bilingual school, and I learned English very quickly, even though the education system labeled me as an ESL (English as a Second Language) student, a label that followed me all the way to sixth grade.

For as long as I can remember, my parents have always praised education as the key to success in life. They must have been speaking this into me from the womb because, in my earliest memory of hearing it, my little brain just went "Yes of course." There was never any doubt that I would try my hardest and place all focus, on this one responsibility: school.

With every worksheet and assignment given to me by the teacher, I was immediately honed in, laser-focused on the instructions given, and enthusiastically going to work. I especially loved any assignment where I could use my crayons, adding color to those boring black-and-white papers was so satisfying. With this focus, I excelled, bringing home worksheets full of stars and happy faces next to praising comments from my teachers. My mother would praise me even more at home, celebrating every star, and so the incentive was set. Throughout my schooling, I consistently brought home papers of recognition: Principal's List, Honor Roll, Student of the Month, Perfect Attendance, and more. I would even refuse to miss a day of school when I was sick, fearing I would fall behind if I wasn't there to hear the instructions.

My drive to succeed in school was further solidified by our

circumstances at home. We always lived paycheck to paycheck. I could see my dad's stress as he hesitantly opened the mail, which only brought bills. My mother was resourceful, shopping at discount stores, getting free resources from church and schools, hosting yard sales, and buying food on sale or in bulk. There was the occasional comment of "Es que no hay dinero," "There is just no money," quickly followed by "Por eso tu tienes que sobresalir para que tengas para todo." "This is why you need to succeed so you can have enough for everything." The worry and stress behind the lack of money in our home had a solution, and that solution was on me, and my success with school.

I kept excelling in school as the years passed, doing the best I could to show my parents, and myself, that there was hope. Then, I completed a very important milestone, I was the first in my family to graduate from high school. It was a joyous moment, for both my parents and me. We cried, we laughed, and the sparkle in my dad's eyes warmed my heart. This accomplishment only fueled me; therefore, I was off to the next goal; college.

Throughout my childhood, I loved to draw. I enjoyed my art classes at school and often gave myself art projects. I would spend hours in my room perfecting an image, drawing and erasing, and then drawing and erasing some more until I was satisfied with my result. I briefly considered going to art school and filled out an assessment test, which brought one of the college admission reps to our home. It was an amazing presentation, but as soon as he showed us the tuition amount, and no real scholarship opportunities, I was heartbroken. I could see myself at this school, but there was no way I would ask my parents for that money. After the rep left, my parents commented that art doesn't really pay well, and that was all the information I needed to move on.

After much research, submission of several scholarship applications, and navigating the tedious and confusing FAFSA paperwork, I was admitted to Arizona State University with grants and a full ride from a Latino scholarship program called "Los Diablos." The grants covered my school supplies, meal plan, and, to my parent's disapproval, my dorm room. As much as I loved our home, the family expectations, the pressure to be the perfect daughter, and my parent's constant stress about bills were becoming overwhelming. As a young woman seeking more freedom and taking on my mother's adventurous spirit, I wanted to experience a different environment.

As I browsed through countless college brochures, my eyes lit up at the images of students in dorm rooms, and the campus life. As a Latina firstborn daughter, I was never allowed to go to sleepovers. I faced strict curfews when going out with friends, and feared disappointing my parents, which often led to anxiety as curfew hour approached. I wanted a life without these limitations, a chance to learn, grow, and experience life detached from my parents. I was ready to leave home. Convincing my parents that living in a dorm was a good idea was a losing battle; no matter how many facts I presented, they still disapproved. However, as much as it pained me to go against their wishes, I was determined to have the full university experience. I felt it in my gut, this was how I was supposed to do it.

One of the "Los Diablos" mentors told me, "These will be the best four years of your life," and they truly were! ASU offered a vibrant campus with hundreds of resources and experiences. I attended club meetings, campus events, and speaker workshops. There were festivals, concerts, movie showings, and exposure to different foods, cultures, and people! The classrooms were intellectually stimulating, and I could not get enough of the conversations with my peers. I took up archery and discovered a stress reliever in salsa dancing. I practiced yoga for the first time and connected with many Latinos on campus. I became a student leader, helping to recruit and retain Latino students, co-founded an activist group defending Mexican labor workers, and even ran for student government on a diverse ticket. I created a colorful newsletter for my Latino peers and loved attending art and design exhibits. A remarkable twist to my college career was being one of three students from campus nominated to attend the CIA conference in Washington D.C., an invitation that only happens every five years. This eye-opening trip is something I will never forget.

As an occasional side hustle, I designed flyers for campus party crews, earning $100 per design to help pay for my groceries. By the end of my university career, I successfully raised money and collaborated with multiple organizations and vendors to create one of the biggest indoor events ever hosted by the multicultural student center, the department that hired me on as a student worker. I created this event to bring much-needed hope and empowerment to my Latino peers, who were distraught over a racist piece of legislation passed in Arizona that affected our undocumented students and the mental health of the Latino student population. It was an amazing campus for me to discover who I was apart from my parents and what I was capable of achieving.

However, as amazing as I was outside of the classroom, it was a struggle inside. While the classes were intellectually stimulating, the textbooks and homework were a challenge. I tried my hardest, yet I could only manage a C+ average, with some semesters a B. One thought that kept running through my mind; was "I won't go back home without completing this." Ultimately, all the hard work paid off when I became the first person in my family to graduate from college. It was a feeling like no other; I had put in the work, sweat, and literal tears for this diploma, and no one could take that away from me.

Then came the real world.

Having graduated in 2009 during a Great Recession, I started selling home security alarms, door-to-door, in the summer heat of Arizona. However, all the skillsets I gained through my experiences on campus came into play. When the marketing director discovered my computing skills, I was able to get out of the heat and start creating marketing material for the company. Soon after, the main office recognized my organizational skills and promoted me to Office

Manager, where I developed effective systems and the company's standard operating procedures. The funding department then noticed my attention to detail and ease with software, leading to my promotion to Funding Manager, where I processed incoming contracts from eight different states. I even assisted with the company's expansion by opening a new office in a different city. All these skills stemmed from my years as a student leader at ASU.

The home security industry provided me with many opportunities. I eventually quit when I hit a ceiling with the company and began freelancing my skills. One amazing opportunity took me to Long Island, New York, to start another office, living in New York had always been on my bucket list! I soaked in the city life for about four months before our contract was unexpectedly terminated due to a leadership conflict. The news came suddenly, with no assistance to fly back home. Thinking I had more time, I hadn't saved any money; I was enjoying nights out in the city and sending money back to my parents. I found myself broke, stranded in a city I barely knew, with no job, and facing homelessness the next day. I owe my safe return home to one of the top salesmen at the company. A friendship that came about easily for me since we were the only ones of Mexican descent in a predominantly Caucasian company. He spent his own money to buy me a flight home and even found me a job to come back to, helping me save face with my parents. This act of kindness is something I will never forget.

From there I never looked back. It was always about moving forward, gaining skills, getting promoted, or finding another company that would pay more. I would have high hopes for each company I entered. However, if the compensation or growth wasn't there, I would leave once I was offered something better. I would change companies almost every year, each time gaining a salary increase. I went from working for a charter school, to a university, to finally landing a job with a Fortune 500 company.

Then I went to work. I moved from an entry-level position to an entry manager, ultimately achieving my goal of becoming a Project

Manager. At this level, I reached a six-figure salary, which initially brought me comfort, but soon came the infamous corporate America golden handcuffs. By this time, I had gained a husband, two boys, two dogs, businesses, a mortgage, and a car note, with my priority being to provide and keep building. However, I began to be depleted, and unfulfilled. I realized that money was no longer a motivator for me; what I truly longed for was fulfillment, but I didn't know how to find it.

In a moment of depression, I turned to coloring, and this activity brought me peace. I would get quiet, and downloads would start coming.

"I should book the free coaching session I have in my membership,"

"I'm going to start journaling again in the mornings,"

"I need to look into self-love."

All these thoughts guided me towards actions that brought me joy and led to a realization; I had suppressed my inner child and focused on the adult world of hard work, recognition, and success. I started to remember my childhood days of using crayons on black and white worksheets, my enjoyment of art classes, the heartbreak over art college, the colorful newsletter I created, the art and design exhibits, and the flyers designed in college. I realized that my feelings of depression began when my employer enforced company-wide Microsoft templates. The Excel sheets and PowerPoints had been my only creative outlets within the corporate world, where I found ways to incorporate images and color. Once that was taken away, that was the last straw, my little creative heart could take.

I had turned away from the joy that came from art and design. Since I had a habit of constant learning, I decided that the next program I would invest in would be related to art. In comes NFTs. I purchased a program about NFTs, a new technology that allowed you to make money from art, which felt like the best of both worlds for me, art and money! I dove in and fell in love.

Entering a world of digital art galleries, innovative artists, and color palettes that only technology could create, NFTs reignited a part of me that had been suppressed for years. They gave me permission to embrace my love for art and allow beauty back into my life. I began supporting Latina artists, galleries, and powerful Latina art, yearning for representation in every space I entered. NFTs provided me the opportunity to accumulate and ultimately own an art asset. I wanted my collection to feature powerful minority women, and soon I had amassed about 50 pieces.

It was through the world of Web3 that I transitioned from NFTs to AI (Artificial Intelligence), opening a whole realm of possibility. Thanks to AI, and creative software platforms like Canva, I can now create whatever my imagination dreams up. For too long, my creative spirit was stifled within corporate America, and within me, was an unstoppable urge to bring to life the images that had been simmering in my mind for over two decades.

Everything that is me began pouring out into these images, as if I had finally allowed a dam of creativity that I had closed off to flow freely. I designed and created what inspired me, and this expression quickly became my brand. I create what I haven't seen before—what makes me feel bold, fierce, and adventurous—and I want that feeling for all of us. I create what I find to be empowering—pieces that embody strength, and resilience, taking up space and color unapologetically. I share my work with the world, hoping it sparks empowerment in others, just as it sparks it in me.

As soon as I started sharing my designs, downloads began to pour in. They seemed to be fulfilling a purpose that time would reveal. As I built my inventory, I received excited comments, questions, and then... requests! I've had the pleasure of creating branding images and merchandise for small Latina business owners, as well as journals, calendars, coloring books, tote bags, stickers, and more. Driven by my love for my community, my search for empowerment, and my passion for art and beauty, the images I've always longed to see are now powerfully adding much-needed Latina representation to our world. My mission has become Latina empowerment in this niche I find myself in.

My journey has taught me to follow my joy, because there is a purpose for you there. Embrace it and cultivate it, for it will ignite you like nothing else. When you shine amiga, your authentic light will give permission for the rest of our hermanas to do the same - and we truly need that for ourselves.

ABOUT DARLENE MENJIVAR

Darlene Menjivar is a 1st generation Latina who was invited to Washington DC for a CIA conference, a creator of organizations, businesses, and a trailblazer within her family. She is the founder of Diosa Legacy, a brand that embodies empowerment, creativity, and Latina representation like no other. She has an adventurous and creative spirit, which was her guiding compass towards her purpose. She spent decades chasing promotions and higher salaries only to realize a 6-figure salary was not fulfilling her like she thought it would.

She's a Latina who loves her parents but has painfully gone against their wishes to embrace the opportunities this country offered her. She serves as a source of wisdom, sought out by those in her network. She has taught others how to budget, embrace self-love, create effective routines, and provide creative solutions; all deriving from her experiences, and love of self-development. Darlene is a full-time worker, business owner, mother of two, wife, daughter, aunt, sister, friend, and perpetual student. She is learning to confide in her resilience and intuition and continues to grow and heal.

Author Page: www.amazon.com/author/diosalegacy
Etsy: www.diosalegacy.etsy.com
Instagram: www.instagram.com/darlene.empower
Business Instagram: www.instagram.com/diosalegacy
Pinterest: www.pinterest.com/diosalegacy

3
LAURA TABAREZ

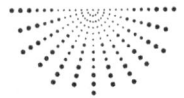

DANCE WITH YOUR HEART

*V*amos a bailar – **wanna dance?** But first, take a minute to be still. Think of nothing else other than your breath and your beautiful heartbeat in harmony. Go ahead and take a couple of minutes, you'll be glad you did. Before diving into the beats of this story, ask yourself, have you ever felt a tug in your heart, urging you to chase your dream or inspiration, asking you out for a dance? Write down one thing that comes to mind and put it aside for now. You see, following your heart isn't just about making bold moves; it's about igniting courage within you that you might not even realize existed. It's that spark that can turn into fuel for your journey. So let me take you to this special place, to a part of my life where Laurita (my childhood nickname) realized how big her heart is, and where I hope inspires you to open up your heart and dance. Thank you in advance for holding the space for my vulnerability.

THE EMERGENCE OF RESILIENCE

I've always loved music. In fact, Laurita was always the one to open up the dance floor at a cumpleanos and any other party. However, this day the beat of my heart felt different. In the middle of the park, only a few steps ahead yet miles away, the music of laughter filled the air with an uplifting hope that was promising. Their giggles mixed with the warmth of the sun and the sweet melodies of birds nearby, you know those tiny ones that circle around super-fast as they bounce from tree to tree, creating a picture-perfect scene of freedom and joy. The little girl with curly hair looked so sweet as she swung back and forth on the monkey bars with no worries in her smile. The young girl in the white overalls climbing towards the top of the slide so gently as to not get her clothes dirty (I assumed), inspired a trickle in my heart of how fun the ride would be. It was such a beautiful sight, full of life and cheer, painting a lovely picture of youth and ease. However, that was not my current reality and feeling in my heart.

For me, it was all about that bench. Oh, that bench was something else. I could still feel the cold and prickly texture of the thorns against my thighs as I looked toward all the displays of joy that I wished I had. The energy dull and heavy from the wear and tear forced to remain strong for the restful moments of its visitors. My fingers twirled around the cold screws that held the bench together. As I sat there on this tired bench, surrounded by all this joy, I felt out of place.

The contrast between my own feelings and the carefree happiness around me seemed to grow wider, leaving me feeling alone and unsettled. I was just a small girl in all the senses of the term, feeling lost in the vastness of life, wrestling with the heavy feelings weighing me down. Those knots in my stomach, heavy with fear and anxiety, were like a physical representation of all the messy emotions swirling inside me—fear, worry, confusion, and a stubborn refusal to give in. They traveled up my throat and hung around restricting the words from flowing effortlessly. I had felt that knot in my throat before (still do sometimes). Those words flew around my mind much like the birds. How did we get here? Why? How? Not fair! Surely this couldn't be the dream we all wished to realize. Why? How?—These were the thoughts that filled my head. Sure, the warm and sunny day was inviting, but I felt myself slipping deeper into a kind of numb sadness, and momentarily detached from the world around me.

I had brought her here, Mi Ama, at that moment before heading back "home," where we sat outside the community park. It was the summer after 5th grade. Something wasn't right in my world—our world—and I'd decided enough was enough. Amidst all the colors and activity in the playground, something really stood out to me—a bright red slide that caught my eye, the one the fearless girl in white overalls committed to tackling. Bold and full of life, it seemed to echo the mix of emotions churning inside me and serve as the beacon for a new challenge that could be—should be—mastered. It was like a mirror reflecting the strength I was finding to face my fears head-on. I could be strong enough to tell her I'm not happy—I got this! Just like that fiery red slide, standing strong amid weathering and buffering the heat to delight the millions of kids that conquered it, I was determined to stand tall. My voice would be heard and would make a difference in my life. I was ready to let her know, I couldn't bear it any longer. I wanted to go back home to Rosarito.

So, I turned over with all the determination and courage that was available to me in that moment. Then, I noticed another beacon drawing my attention—Los Ojos de mi 'Ama (My Mom's eyes). The closer I looked into her eyes, I saw a reflection of my own fears and struggles. I was digging in deep for those answers to the questions in my head. I remember her clearly, "Que? Que paso? (What? What happened)," as she asked anxiously, but my thoughts kept spinning as my eyes softened by the moisture that would soon burst out— Where were those visions, I knew for sure would come to reality here in the United States. "Te acuerdas Ama? Que Paso?" With my wonder piercing into her eyes, I attempted to bring her along to my long-yearned visions that fueled my passion and excitement in the summer of 1986, the year I was brought to the US. I began to share my visions of how I thought life might be here with our "family" I told her that I'd constructed daydreams of a future that drew from all sorts of beautiful scenarios.

I imagined myself in the busy center of a rich Californian city, Sacramento, in my mind bigger than the world itself, and just over the gates of the scary Tijuana highway, complete with the steady chatter of the luxurious English language that I had mastered and embarked on the pursuit of shiny opportunities, the "American Dream"– mi corazon filled with curiosity.

My dreams were also filled with visions of success—such as becoming the well-dressed lady in the bank, owning the room with purpose and elegance, that me and mi Abuelita met when we went to set up the bank account for the financial abundance that would sure come my way. And the smell of the homemade tortillas my Nana placed on the mesa (table). Or driving a sleek car much like the one in which my Tia would occasionally pick me up in for our shopping trips, matching boots and all. Or that of a beautiful home filled with flowers such as the vivero (nursery) mi Ama spent many of her teenage years working before migrating to the US. Most of all, I would come here and learn so much in a world where I can create all the happiness one can think of. How was it that I came to experience the complete opposite since my arrival filled with memories of abuse in ALL of the senses one could think of?

I shared with her the abuse that I'd experienced and seen over the years, the sexual abuse and trauma that still haunted me in the nights, the fear and anxiety that she or one of my siblings be beaten again, the weakness I felt in feeling out of my place in our own "home," the embarrassment I felt when my peers picked on me at school, the frustration I felt because I didn't sign up for this. WE didn't sign up for this. I was lost, afraid, and alone. The rich California city I imagined had become cold and uninviting.

My mind was no longer filled with curiosity about prosperity, instead, it housed feelings of resentment and confusion. I wondered if the well-dressed lady at the bank had suffered all this pain before her success and if it was worth it? Family dinners were not filled with warm tortillas at the table, but rather of loneliness and yearning for her to come back from work. I no longer had anyone that would pick up me for fun shopping trips as we shared our dreams for the future. The flower beds I'd imagined we'd had at home were there, but I had to look through them through gated windows. I wanted to go back home, back to a place where I was free to wander and where without any riches, I had the biggest of hearts that could shine bright. A place where my voice was heard, and my dreams meant something. My tears were overflowing as if I'd never cried before cold and unwelcomed. I just didn't belong here.

Yet, the understanding that resonated with me the most at that moment was that my sharing my experience made her feel even weaker, unable to take the action she knew my heart was inspiring her to take. She, too, was defenseless. Her tears were just as strong as mine. I couldn't even start to think of what was going on in her head, but I knew that we wouldn't leave. MY protector, migrating herself to an unknown city at the age of twenty and with three kids, was unequipped to guard us from the harsh realities that sought to scar our lives, irreparably. There was no going back, Laura. Here in Sacramento is where we'd make our home. Sure enough, "Ok Mija, no nos vamos, pero algo va a cambiar."

You see by this time we had both experienced abuse, and while she may not have been able to stand up for herself, I had had enough. We shared a silent understanding through those eyes, a recognition of the hardships we both faced. It was like we were in this together, grappling with the pain and loneliness that life had thrown our way. Each glance was a shared prayer, a silent cry for help, adding yet another layer to our shared narrative.

Through everything, however, her eyes also reflected a strength that mirrored mine. They held the promise of collective resilience — a reiteration of my determination, our determination, to never surrender to the hands of abuse. The connection sealed. She didn't see a way to take us back home, but would soon share with me a critical part of my history that would eventually bring me back to my authentic self. That day in the park, that bright red promise of the slide became a resemblance of my heart speaking directly to me and inspiring me to push on. Not only to push on for myself but also to be the beacon for my mother, so that we could still make those bright dreams a reality. She was unable to shield us from the pain that we'd already endured, but my heart didn't allow me to be swayed that those dreams would no longer be attainable. I knew there was something bigger within us.

Something bigger within me and in my heart. I stood tall and bright, and, in that moment, red became my favorite color—a reminder that there is a strength within me, a dance, that is unexplainable yet powerful. In that moment, I understood that mi Ama did her best. That moment marked the inception of a role reversal, which I later recognized as parentification and the resilience that emerged from it. We left the park together walking down the rough streets of Oak Park, realizing that we'd just made a decision to thrive. I mean come on ya'll after many therapy sessions later in life, I realized I'd taken on so much. Now was it fair?? No! But that was my reality, and my dance in that moment. The color red would for a long time become my shield, protector, and calling for God's presence and the Angels that have surrounded me since. While we wouldn't be going back to Rosarito, from that day on I never experienced or witnessed any more abuse in our home, and neither did she. The years following were filled with dances of many genres....

VAMOS A BAILAR! -EMBRACING RESILIENCE

Since arriving in California, I quickly learned to speak on behalf of my parents in a world they couldn't navigate without me. My half-spoken English carried the weight of our worlds—scheduling doctor's appointments, attending school meetings, and trying to understand the intricacies of financial responsibilities as I helped keep the family bills paid. It was a crash course in adulthood, one that I took on with unwavering commitment.

My siblings became my world. My heart vowed to not only care and protect them, but also be the best role model I could be. I'd escaped the abuse ever since the day at the park and took on the new responsibility of being a caregiver before I was a teenager. Weekdays were the best because we were at school most of the days, where I could stay in the classroom learning all day long if I could have it my way. The weekends were mostly long because we ended up moving around, and I didn't have many friends. However, by the time I was in sixth grade, my mom surprised me with one of the best gifts ever, my family history and a meeting with my biological father.

The story is for another time, but the day I met him changed my life forever and gave me a glimpse of what a home really felt like. By the time I was in high school, after moving around several times, I'd experienced many more spurts of resilience as I helped to care for my siblings, making bad choices when I was alone because I was lost still trying to figure out who I would be here in the US, half my time trying to keep up with American culture and half keeping up with telenovelas and my favorite bandas. I picked up drinking alcohol for a bit too trying to self-medicate from the childhood trauma that would pop up from time to time leaving me feeling lost and confused in a place where it didn't feel like my own.

The summers were amazing because I got to go back home and spend the time in Rosarito. During those times when I experienced loneliness in high school, I found solace in learning, writing, and spending time with the first love of my life who would later become my husband. I had found a couple of solid friends, and they were my rocks. I had other friends in school too, but they never knew about my childhood and the adversity I'd faced. By this time, I found a new me to focus on—someone who was more aligned with her heart and the inner child within her. As my graduation grew close, my dreams and visions of that once bright future in California became yet again a reality for me.

By the time I was a junior, I vowed to create the "American Dream" for myself and to be a role model for my mom and my siblings—a home filled with love and joy. During those years, I leaned into my heart many many times to help me align on what felt good, for the inspiration and drive towards a goal, and to pull courage when I needed it, remembering that fierce red slide. It wasn't easy, I had a lot of healing to do (and still heal every day). I vowed to the girl in the mirror—who once carried the world on her shoulders—that I would pursue those dreams of literature and learning, that I'd live out those visions I imagined and daydreamed about as a little girl in Rosarito.

I understand now that the responsibilities I bore were not merely chains but the threads weaving the tapestry of my identity because I still had my heart that sang to me with the right dance at the right time, and on which I could always count. Going straight to college from high school was not possible, financially or logistically, but that would remain in my heart. Instead, I moved out at the age of eighteen and decided to make business my choice of career and follow my dream of being in leadership roles and creating the financial freedom that would allow me to have the perfect marriage, home, and life. Oh boy! Would the courage to dance with my heart continue to show up....

LA RUTA DEL CORAZON: LET YOUR HEART LEAD THE WAY

My knees met the ground with a soft thud, the force of gravity cradling me as that familiar knot in my throat reappeared. I was six months pregnant, filled with all the joy I'd felt in my entire life. But as I met the ground, the feeling of emptiness in my stomach was overtaking. I was, yet again, alone and afraid. The minutes felt like hours as I lay there, cradling my beautiful belly filled with love. The texture of the carpet grazed my fingers, grounding me, pulling me back from the swirling vortex of what was supposed to be. We had it ALL. Together, we had traveled, soaked up new experiences, and returned bursting with tales and laughter, only for me to wake alongside him on this day and realize that our lives were going in different directions as his heart yearned for something else.

In my mind, we'd built our perfect home and marriage and many of my childhood dreams had come to realization, the perfect car, the perfect career, the perfect family filled with laughter and dancing our way through life—no fresh tortillas because cooking is just not my thing. I remember once the guys, my husband, and brothers, caught that we were making enchiladas with rotisserie chicken, it was the funniest thing!

Our family get-togethers are filled with amazing memories because over the years my family and his family had become one. We pretty much did everything together (my brothers/sisters and his). He was my best friend, was the first person in my teenage years I could trust with my heart and love. We had the perfect family car (Nissan Murano) picked out, we'd moved to a safer place to raise our perfectly-planned-for-this-world and amazing son, Andres. I was on the fast track to becoming a district manager for my organization AND only one class away from becoming a court reporter where I'd planned to start my business slowly with contract depositions. Yeah, I can type 220 WPM, it was on a steno machine, but still, it was going to become such a fun and intriguing career. All the hard work and determination was beginning to pay off, and I was ready to ride another fun wave of dreams coming to fruition.

However, in that moment, the questions started swirling in my head just like they did that day in the park—How did we get here? Why? How? Not fair! Surely this couldn't be the dream we all wished to realize. But this time the voices in my heart were stronger. You see, in my heart, I knew that he was meant for something else. Those moments in our marriage when I should have 'known' that we wouldn't be together and that his heart would go astray, I ignored because I was so set on not letting this life filled with the security, love, and family I so yearned for when I first came to California. I was prepared to fight for it, and I did for many years.

I still remember the rough feeling of that carpet, the tears along my cheeks and throat that felt as cold as they did that day in the park. We were going in different directions because his heart called out for more, and my heart also told me with a faint but audible whisper, "You will also grow and find more." And so, I vowed to listen. I picked myself up, powered by the knowing in my heart and the love for my baby, and asked that we go somewhere and talk about how we would make this work. Shortly after he moved out and we welcomed our precious baby to this world, Andres. We would figure out how to co-parent and still be the best of friends, and I would get my career back on track in some way. The next few years were very hard... but I eventually I found a way to listen even closer and dance with my heart...

DE MI CORAZON, AL TUYO – FROM MY HEAR TO YOURS

Ok now let's go back look at that note that you wrote and hold that thought of what your heart is calling you to do. You see, the individual tapestries of young Latina immigrants are woven with distinct threads—each pattern unique to circumstances such as socioeconomic background, immigration motivations, childhood and family upbringing, community support, and personal strengths. Though they may be scarred by trials such as parentification and trauma, as was mine, or not, these patterns bear the potential for remarkable strength, familial intimacy, and an enriched outlook on life. I think it's important to recognize that such adversities should not dictate the full narrative of a person's path. Through the lens of my own narrative, punctuated with challenges yet speckled with joy and love as grand as el corazón de mi Ama, I have drawn strength to refashion hardships into stepping-stones towards fulfilling my deepest aspirations. This transformation into a heart-led existence wasn't an impromptu epiphany. It required a gradual alignment of conviction and support—a symphony of inherited and shared dreams waiting to be orchestrated by my heart's desires.

Indeed, I stood out in my family for achieving many firsts and achieving the "American Dream"—a traditional Catholic marriage, purchasing a home, six-figure incomes, several corporate roles, entrepreneurial successes, and academic accolades—but these achievements were not solely my own. They were manifestations of ancestral melodies longing for expression. Attuned to these legacies and my heart, I surrounded myself with a chorus of supporters—family, friends, mentors—who believed in me tirelessly. I have a career that I have paved based on my values and strengths, a business that fills my heart, the freedom to go back home to my roots often, and have raised an amazing son that I am SO proud of! The pivotal moment came when coaching revealed itself to me. My coach did not just offer strategies; she provided a mirror for self-reflection, enabling me to attune to my inner voice and listen even closer to my Corazon. Together, we crafted a vision filled with the music of my heart, giving rhythm to my steps forward.

I extend these harmonies to you. Let your heart lead your dance, and boldly step into the life you envision. Follow that nudge your heart called at the beginning of this story. The resilience to thrive amid cultural or systemic struggles is within you—a legacy that is alive in every heartbeat. Lean in, listen closely, and let the pulse of your desires guide your journey. You are exactly where you need to be right now to have acquired all the right experience to drive you forward. It is never too late and the nudge within your heart is there if you will only take the time to listen. Dance to the rhythm your heart plays and trust it to lead you to joy and fulfillment. Vamos a bailar?

ABOUT LAURA TABAREZ

Laura Tabarez, a first-generation Latina immigrant and dedicated Mom, draws from her growth over childhood and cultural challenges to inspire success, resilience, and heart-based living in both corporate and coaching sectors. Inspired by her service on the frontlines, she adeptly evolves customer experience strategies within the corporate world, bolstering frontline capabilities. Concurrently, as a Leadership & Empowerment Coach, she equips clients with dynamic tools to master their career obstacles and create a heart-based life. Laura's multifaceted expertise not only advocates personal advancement but also mirrors her victorious battle against early adversities, fueling her passion for helping others break through their own barriers and intentionally co-create a meaningful reality while maintaining integrity to their authentic values.

Laura has a B.A. in Business Leadership, an MS in I/O Psychology, project management and professional coaching certifications, and a mission to empower professionals to navigate their career with confidence and meaning. She inspires leaders and changemakers to act from their heart and promote resilience and transformation.

Website: www.coachingwithlaura.com
Email: laura@coachingwithlaura.com
LinkedIn: www.linkedin.com/in/lauratabarez
Facebook: www.facebook.com/coachlauratabarez
YouTube: www.youtube.com/@coachlauratabarez

4
LIZETTE ROMO

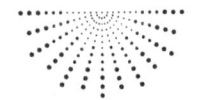

CHANGE THE NARRATIVE

*L*et me start by saying I am not a writer. I am just sharing my heart in written words in the hopes that you might resonate with something in this chapter. And more importantly, that you might have a few takeaways that encourage you to stand in your power and purpose, despite how your family, or people in general may have made you feel. It took me a long time to find my power and my voice, but I am here now. I'll just remind you as you read this chapter; Eres valiente, poderosa y inteligente. Post those words everywhere as a reminder to yourself. Let's get into it.

I grew up in a neighborhood filled with working-class minority families just trying to survive. Each day was a struggle, and despite working families being on the grind, generational poverty and a scarcity mindset were common. Most families in our neighborhood had two or three generations in the same house. We were no different. When my grandmother bought the house, the white residents at the time protested. Back then, the propaganda posted everywhere was "no Mexicans, Indians or dogs."

The people that lived there were angry because they considered brown people low class. As if the Americas weren't completely colonized?! It was just how it was back then. Years later, the signs were no longer posted and civil rights were at the forefront. Small progress. Sadly, we still perpetuate some of this same behavior in our own community through colorism and classism. You've probably heard the term "No seas Indio," or familiar nicknames like guera, morenita, no sabo in Spanish, and plenty more in English. Those little jabs that can be disguised as loving terms are painful sometimes. Probably painful like what my grandmother experienced just trying to buy her first home. I think we need to break that cycle, regardless of how endearing those terms may be. They can hurt, just a little.

In my neighborhood, our moms were all beautiful, vibrant chingonas who were barely 18 or 19. Most of them had no fathers around. Our mothers were basically kids themselves and living their lives. And despite us having other family members around in our homes, all of us neighborhood kids were a little feral and out running the streets. We roamed the neighborhood like a gang looking for something to get into. Since everyone knew our families, people in the neighborhood would snitch us off and we'd get beat. We did not care about the beating we would get later. Oh yeah, we were brave until that belt came out or the chancla flew! Like many kids in our generation, we played outside until the streetlights came on, and never once thought about checking in.

In our house, you could always find beans and rice on the stove in the kitchen regardless of what the main meal was. There wasn't much else, but those foods were comforting and familiar. It was normal. The comal was always ready on the stove for the next batch of goodness whether it was tortillas or frybread which tastes like a sope. My uncles would often sit at the kitchen table, drink, and talk smack to each other and about everyone else. They would sit there and see who could eat the hottest chile.' I thought they were crazy sitting there all sweaty, gross, laughing, eating, and drinking. When I saw them at the table, I would sprint the other way! I had been tricked too many times with them saying come here ...it's not hot! Damn chumps, they were always messing with me.

Besides the constant comfort foods, I remember our house was always filled with people. Beautiful brown people. Family, friends, and activists. Conversations were passionate around brown pride, Indigenous rights, and preserving our culture. I thought it was so cool. It's a great memory. But it also reminds me how much of an outsider I felt like growing up. Why you ask? I wasn't born with beautiful brown skin like my mother. I have a European father and I came out like a damn fluorescent highlighter with white skin, black hair, and hazel-green eyes. I swear, genetics are so damn unpredictable! So here I was, this little fluorescent child in a household of beautiful brown people.

That's not uncommon, we come in all colors. But when I was little, I'd get sat in a chair, baby oil slathered on, and left to sit outside for hours to "get some color." And we wonder why we have complexes?! That always felt like such a chore. I'd get golden beige, but never as dark as I'm sure she might have liked. At least that's what it felt like to me. And after hours in the sun, with only a little "color" it always felt like I failed the mission. Can you imagine feeling like a failure for something like that as a kid? It makes me laugh just thinking about how ridiculous society and our own community of colorism can be. The hot days in the sun just perpetuated me feeling more out of place in my own home. I don't blame her for the sun-capades, but it was a source of shame that I carried for years.

Back in the day, my mom (aka her crew as peewee) and her crew would hit up the cruise on the weekends and hang out at the local restaurants doing what street kids do. There, she eventually hooked up with my donor. I call him my donor because that's really all he was. He was a good-looking, self-centered womanizer who cared about women and his precious Chevy Impalas more than anything else. My mom just happened to be one of many that got caught up.

My donor wasn't around, didn't provide any support, and was a deadbeat. I was her problem to deal with. Maybe that resonates with you? I'm sorry if it does. Because of that, my mom worked 6 and 7 days a week to survive. Instead of my mom being my caretaker, whoever was at the house got to "look out" for me.

Most of the time, I didn't want to be at my own house without her. My tios used to tell me to sit in the closet because my fluorescent skin was blinding them. Or they would make me sit on the porch and "wait for my real family" to pick me up. Then, they would come get me off the porch after a few hours, laugh, and drink some more. I guess we all project trauma at some point onto others, especially family. I felt very alone all the time & I wanted to run away. But where would I go? Weakness got you a beating, and you weren't allowed to talk to people about your feelings. You just sucked it up. We are taught to be grateful & keep quiet. I wanted to tell my mom what went on, but I could always hear the tone of disappointment if I did. Basically, telling me to stop crying about nothing. They don't mean it.

So here I was, a little fluorescent kid in a family I felt I didn't belong in. And my identity was shaped by a lens that didn't match the color of my skin. So confusing. Brown kids experience the opposite when they are told not to go in the sun too much, so they don't get too dark. What?! I swear society is just a damn mess.

When I was seven, a new form of trauma came. My mom had a homeboy named Robert. These two were tight. They had a whole crew, but these two were always running the streets and looking out for each other. He used to watch me when my mom needed him to. He gave me my first crucifix and was always showering me with presents. He didn't baptize me, but he may as well have been my godfather because before the molestation facts came out, she used to say if something happened to her he'd take me.

One day she asked him to keep me overnight. He decided he had the right to touch me that night. And that began a long torment that I don't wish on anyone. I desperately wanted to tell someone to help me and make it stop, but I was afraid of the response. He was tight with our whole Familia. Tight like he may as well have been de la misma sangre, type of tight. Soon after, I started giving excuses when my mom wanted me to go there. Pleading to stay home by myself or go to the neighbors. But I had to go there more times than I want to remember.

After a few years, I finally got up the courage to speak up. There was a party for something at the house, and with everyone there, I saw an opportunity to have the Familia come to my rescue. I just knew it would be an immediate ass beating for this puto. I was so wrong. I was told I was lying, and how could I say that?! Stop making up stories, they said. I was devastated. I cried so much and felt the shame come down like a brick. I didn't go back there, which also told me they knew I wasn't lying. Did anyone apologize, hug me, and say it will be ok? No. No one did anything because we don't talk about those things in our community. Until my prima spoke up to her parents about him doing the same thing! I wish I could say I felt vindicated, but I didn't. It was just another block up for the wall of generational trauma. He was arrested and it was a long trial that we had to recount details on, and he ended up going to prison.

A few years later, we moved to a new hood. Same old thing. Rough neighborhood, working families dealing with poverty, drugs, alcohol and gangs. Middle school was alright, and I was just trying to stay away from home by joining clubs. But, by the time I got to 9th grade, I linked up with my forever homegirls. They were a light in my life! Jessica, Patty & Tricia were my ride or dies. With our big hair (thank you, Aqua net), eyeliner, and hoops you couldn't tell us anything. By this time, I had added some extra-curricular activities to my life after we moved. It was called running the streets, skipping school, and getting into fights. Why not? What else should I do? I had something to prove, and I was down for whatever, if it meant showing how hardcore I was. That's what mattered in our hood. If you would throw down with people when the shit jumped off. I mean in fairness; my mom ran with her crew and made her bones that same way. Cycles are what they are right?

I was just out doing dumb shit. Stole a few cars, and tossed some things in the river for a few bucks. I had to watch my grades though. I didn't need any letters from school drawing attention. Plus, I liked learning, and I figured out I could benefit from it. You need an assignment done? $10.00. That was ok, but I needed more income, so I started working an after-school job. I'm not proud of it, but I left many a kickback and went straight to work. Yep, under the influence. I was so angry at the world so whatever. Years passed and we got closer to graduation. Although I was working, I had no real direction. I was destined to be stuck in the same cycle as generations before me if I didn't do something. I could hear my family saying, "You better not get pregnant!"

Just before my 18th birthday, I left the house and stayed with a friend while I finished my last few months of school. Even though I had a job I was starving, but I did not care. I had a studio, with my homegirl as a roommate. I spent my free time walking around thinking of side hustles. I wanted to live a life that was not "barely getting by" and just being grateful to have a job. I respect that and there is nothing wrong with it, it's how we are raised. Just be grateful. But I wanted to look back one day and say against all odds. I made it. I broke the cycle, on my own. I don't need anyone. Well, it wasn't easy as I found out. I was naïve, but I was determined to do something different. I wish I could say I chose the path of breaking the generational trauma and poverty cycle for some grandiose reason. But honestly, it was more out of anger & spite than anything.

My mom did her best, and I don't fault her for that. But I believe she could have done more for herself to get out of the generational trauma, and not passed it on. I was determined to show all the people who made me feel "less than" that I had value and didn't need anyone. To show the ones who said I would never amount to anything that they were wrong. I kept working my minimum wage job but showing up hard to get recognized. I didn't know what a leader was, but I had hustle. I earned a few small increases, but they weren't enough to really make a difference.

I decided to hustle up a few bucks to enroll in our local Junior college. I'd take classes around my work schedule. I figured even at 6 units a semester I was making progress. I did this for two years and let me tell you it was tough. I had been elevated to a "manager" position at the place I was working and that added a lot of responsibility. So, I dropped out. Shocker, right?! I justified it in my head as it's for rich people anyway. I know how to hustle. I wish I had just gotten an AA. I didn't know it then, but I could have used that in the future. I knew little about how finances worked, but I was good at math, so I started making my come-up plan. A few years later I had gotten married and had my son. He was the best gift I ever received. He changed my heart in an instant and I knew I had to make something of myself for his sake.

But I was still a kid myself, with a lot of trauma. I divorced his dad in just a few years and found myself as a single mom. Luckily, not for long. I reconnected with a friend from middle school (now my current husband) who would support and love me in a way that I needed for the next stage of life. We have been together for 24 years and he is my biggest supporter and my best friend. Gracias a Dios, he works in mysterious ways. We put him at the center of our marriage, and he blessed us beyond what words can ever describe. Shortly after we got married, God opened a door for my career journey. I had the opportunity to join a construction company as a Project assistant at a real office.

When I stepped foot in that office, I wanted to run back out immediately. I was greeted by the receptionist, and I was immediately hit with imposter syndrome. I don't belong here. Everyone who passed by while I waited to be interviewed was professional, well-dressed, and seemed to speak like politicians. Funny how we can feel small in an unfamiliar environment right? I showed up there thinking I was dressed well, with creases in my pants, my hair perfectly feathered out & high with hoops on with my shiny shoes.

Where I come from, my look was fly. But looking at them, I looked like a poor thug! It's funny to think about it today. This was the first semi-"corporate" environment I had ever been in. Let me tell you, that interview was intense. I was sweating just trying to speak clearly, not use street slang, and avoid looking nervous. A week later they called to offer me the job. I was so juiced!! It was a big salary jump, with better benefits. That was a win.

I did my best to lay low and just work. There were some nice people, and some real stuck-up ones. The first thought in my head was I would love to throw down, on one of these presumidas and scare the shit out of them. I know that's terrible, but it's what it is. I knew had to get calm real fast if I was going to make it. I was an outsider and I needed to learn to operate in their world. Construction was so interesting to me. The fast pace, the differences in each project, and everything about it excited me! But, I felt so out of place in that office. The way I spoke, and carried myself was still very Chicana streetfighter. Haha.

Luckily, about two weeks after I started a young lady came over and introduced herself. To my surprise, I saw someone who looked like me & talked like me! Patti, a Chicana from "209" had been there for about a year. She immediately showed me the ropes and told me who was cool and who to stay away from so I wouldn't get caught up. I was so relieved! As time went on, she and I talked about how we could run circles around all these biased & privileged white men. Many times, we both had to bite our lips because the disparaging comments about Mexicans & every other minority were thrown out on the regular. I'm sure someone reading this has been there and felt powerless to stand up.

Or maybe it was just me. Who knows. Were both white passing and I'm of course part guera anyway, so they never thought twice about saying things in front of us. It was frustrating, but we needed our jobs, so we stayed quiet. We'd go get lunch at this place called El Puerto, and just talk about how to get upward mobility and how much we wanted to tell them where to shove it. We had ambitions!

Patty moved on after a few years & I was slowly being promoted. But I knew I wasn't getting the pay. It was no secret. At the time, I didn't exactly know how to push in and get what I was earning. So, I focused on sponging up every ounce of learning and development I could get. I still had some side hustles, and I was determined to elevate past a "support" role. But back then construction was still a good ol' boy network. Without a college pedigree, an advocate, or being a white man, the door for upward mobility was basically non-existent. I worked on changing the way I carried myself at work and started reading leadership books. I listened to leaders' language and practiced public speaking at any chance I got.

Soon the owners were coming to me for all their projects to run and I was on interview teams for new projects. It was a good experience, and I felt secure. But, if you have ever seen the movie Hidden Figures where the women Engineers do all the work and put someone else's name on the report, that was me. I felt like I had to change everything about who I was, and that was frustrating. After doing that for a while, I approached one of the owners and asked how do I move up to Project Manager. His first response was "Start by not acting like a gangbanger." Say what? I thought I had refined my appearance & speech enough to blend in. Ok, game on. I can put on a corporate suit from 8-5 puto.

Like I said, I was still very volatile inside. Long story short, I did become a project Manager, and then went all the way up to Vice President. I am sure, if I was not a whitexican, that climb would have been much slower. Like I said, society is a mess. But as I grew older, I couldn't deal with the racial bias and patriarchy. My future no longer looked right there and after 12 years, it was time to bounce. I was confident in my skills and had built a strong reputation in the industry. I went out and found a new home. It was emotional and scary, but I was ready. I ended up joining another construction firm of similar size. I had to take a small step back in position and had zero tenure, but I didn't care. And from the day I stepped foot inside, I was treated with respect and could feel the humility and appreciation for employees from the owners. I showed up as my authentic self on day 1. A Chicana, who wore big hoops and big heels and KNEW MY SHIT. I don't mean that in a cocky way, but I was 40 and had finally decided it was time to break the rules of conformance. It was time to step into my power and pull that ripcord.

To my surprise, the owners embraced my Chicana-ness and sincerely embraced my authenticity of self. I could speak Spanish in the office, and just do my thing. They were happy to hear my ideas in whatever way I conveyed them and gave me room to contribute without the need to change my words. I was beyond grateful to Diosito for closing the other door and opening this one. I ended up leaving this company for a season to take another step in my journey toward my goal of becoming an executive. It was hard to leave the people. But, I had an opportunity to join an international GC firm. I knew I needed to work for a larger firm to see a different side of construction. When that opportunity came, I grabbed it. I loved it and learned so much. But I still had a fire in my heart to reach the goal of ownership and opening doors for young women. And according to God's timing, he opened that door back at the firm I had loved.

My first day back, there was a Chingona I couldn't wait to see. Seeing her face made me so happy. It was like no time had passed. I am now a partner and one day will move into taking over the company when the founder retires. What a blessing, no? Being able to lead in such a way that people can be their authentic selves, embrace their cultures, and experience mine is such a gift. It makes me smile and warms my heart when non-Latinas / Latinos in our office make an effort to engage me in Spanish.

It's come full circle, and I am grateful every day. Even for the trauma, because it made me push harder. I get the opportunity to foster a safe environment for people to show up as their authentic selves, we celebrate culture, our differences, and are passionate about continuous improvement for the good of our people. Not just for Latinas & Indigenous women, but everyone. I get to represent us and I'm aware of the responsibility I have to open doors that used to be closed to us. And yes, it's very rewarding when young Latinas & Indigenous women message me and say thank you, you inspire me. Love how you represent us, or thank you for speaking at this event, you encouraged me. Please keep going. We are changing the narrative. She se puede.

ABOUT LIZETTE ROMO

Determined to break free from living out the same addiction and poverty cycles as generations before her, Lizette journeyed a long road to becoming a Senior Executive and Construction company owner, leader, and mentor. She is passionate about elevating people, opening doors, and setting an example of leadership that embraces diversity and creates a safe space for people to contribute as their authentic selves. She is an advocate for DE&I having experienced firsthand the inequality that comes with being in a historically white male-dominated industry. The industry is slowly changing, but there is still work to do. Today, she serves on several industry boards and as a guest board member for companies needing outside input for strategic planning. She's also spoken at construction industry events and as a guest speaker for the Sacramento Hispanic Professional Engineers. Her passion lies in serving others and developing pathways for students to enter the construction industry, especially those from marginalized communities like her own.

She is married to her best friend, Enrique and together they raised four sons. They now have 2 granddaughters and hope there are more on the way. She and her husband are now empty nesters, love to play at different golf courses, seek out great restaurants around their region for date nights, attend Latino & Indigenous cultural events around the region, and spend time in the neighborhood walking the dog.

Website: www.intech-mech.com

5
MARIA MOLINA MONROY

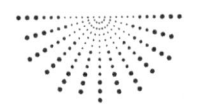

BERRACAS LATINAS!!! BADASS LATINAS!!!

When was the last time you journaled about your most harrowing life experiences? The generational traumas that your parents and grandparents weren't able to break free from. The ones that you have repeated not because you didn't want to have a better life than your ancestors, but perhaps because you didn't feel as though it was in your control. If your answer is never, then you are not alone. This is my first time expressing my deepest generational chains in writing. The chains that expected me to relive my ancestors' life rather than the life I was meant to live. I'm finally giving myself the gift of healing and I know that I will forever be changed for having said yes to sharing my story. Listo! Respire profundo! Ready! Deep breath.

My most favorite childhood memory was from the early 70s when my family was living in an apartment building on 144th Street across the street from Public School 82 in Queens, NY. We lived in a very diverse neighborhood and during the summers, you could hear loud music playing from the apartment windows. It was so loud that you could hear the music from the street level to the rooftop. Vicente Fernández was pretty popular with his song El Rey, Willie Colón with his Salsa La Murga, and the Bee Gees. You also heard Soca and Reggae music. Maybe that's why I listen to a variety of genres and love to dance. On the weekends, my sister and I would join the neighborhood kids running around the illegally opened fire hydrant as if it were a water park. It was super fun, probably not safe, and definitely illegal but common.

Our fun time was limited to 30 minutes and God forbid you weren't back in 30 minutes or you didn't ask permission for more time—Mami would show up like Batman out of the blue and yell at us to get inside. For some reason, it felt like she didn't want us to have fun, and the only way we got permission to play was if we completed the chores. I was still young enough that I didn't really have chores, but my older sister Pat had to cook, clean, and take care of me. Even though play time had to be earned, it was one of my favorite memories because it was just fun playing with my sister.

My parents and my 7-year-old sister arrived in New York in 1970 with a few other family members. As we all know, they came to America for a better life—to live that American dream—the dream that was seeded in my dad's heart after serving in the Korean War as part of the United Nations Command alongside the U.S. in the early 1950s. His dream became a reality and shortly after arriving in the U.S., he was hired as a bodyman, fixing the exterior of cars, and my mother as a seamstress. According to my sister, things were going well for them. They were both employed, of course the language barrier was pretty challenging, but they managed to communicate through finger-pointing. My father had no education and was working in the farms at age 3 and my mother only had 2nd grade education, so the fact they were able to land jobs was a real blessing.

In late 1972, mi Abuelita se enfermo y mi mamá se fue a Colombia. Shortly after returning to NY, she became pregnant with me. While she was happy, my father was not happy. He wanted her to get an abortion probably because he already had five kids from his previous marriage. My mother said she was keeping me even if it meant my dad leaving his family—which he did. He abandoned us leaving my mom and my sister to fend for themselves in a country they knew very little about and spoke little to no English. They suffered through scarcity.

There wasn't enough money to buy food because the rent for the small room with a folding twin bed where my mom and sister slept took priority. As a seamstress, she was paid at piece rate and simply didn't make much money. Things became even more depressing when my mother was let go from her job because her pregnancy was a workplace hazard. Back in those days, pregnant women couldn't work. Pero mi mami no se dio por vencida. My mother did not give up although she could have given me up for adoption to my cousin who proposed the idea, and she said no. She would find a way forward, and so she did.

Thanks to people's generosity including Mami Hortencia--my aunt and cousins who would visit on Sundays with a bag of food, the school lunch ladies who gave Pat extra lunch to take home for dinner, and la Señora Nelly. They helped get them through the dark times they were living. La Señora Nelly was my mom's earth angel. She hired a seven-month-pregnant woman as a seamstress when no one else would. Nelly's heart poured love and care into my mom and sister giving them hope that things would be okay. She would often send a plate of food for my mother and sister to eat dinner. The food was filling, but the love and hope was even more so. She allowed my mother to sew clothes for my sister because there wasn't enough money to buy them.

After I was born, my mother continued working at la Señora Nelly's house where I would go every day. She didn't have the luxury of taking maternity leave or simply being home taking care of me. She had to get right back to work, and I had to come along. I was a Winter baby, so the cold snow days were even harder as la Señora Nelly lived up top of the hill, and pushing the stroller in the snow was a job of its own. How is it that the chains were literally weighing my mother down and yet she kept moving forward facing the hill that life placed in her path?At the age of 4, my parents reunited. I was so happy to have my dad in my life. He could no longer deny my existence thanks to DNA testing. My dad and I soon became best friends. He was kind, caring and soft-spoken.

Growing up, we didn't have much by way of material things but I had my family and that was important to me. There was a sense of security that came with having my family together. Soon after, my dad bought his first casa in Queens Village and things were good. Sure, my parents had their arguments, and my mother was super strict, but wasn't every family like that. Our family gathered every weekend. Sometimes we went to Mami Hortencia's casa, other times we went to my cousin's casa and sometimes everyone would come to our casa.

Our family get-togethers always involved cerveza, whiskey, cigarillos, musica, chistes y risas. These gatherings would feel like fiestas, so much so that I learned how to strike a match and hold my arm steady for others to light up their cigarettes. There's a picture capturing this very scene with my dad. Crazy to think that was a Kodak moment. Well, it wouldn't be a complete story if I didn't share that my mother had my sister lighting up her cigarette and having to inhale a few puffs before passing it back to her. Oddly, but maybe not surprising, I began to eat the tips of the matches, and it wasn't a one-time thing. I would hide under the dining room table to eat the matches as if no one would see me. The moment I was caught my mother rushed me to the hospital because in her mind I had poisoned myself.

Apparently, the matches in the U.S. were safe to eat. According to my mother, it would've been a different story eating matches in Colombia. Matches had an interesting taste. It wasn't sweet or spicy, it had a rough tasty texture and a smoky taste. I can't say with certainty why I did this, but maybe I thought this was my way of smoking since everyone else was doing it.

The weekend drinking became an uncontrollable act for my parents and family alike becoming intoxicated and fights between my parents would break out. As a little six-year-old, all I could feel was anxiety and fear. Anxiety would settle in every Thursday and biting my nails was my coping mechanism. The fear would arrive Friday and would temporarily leave on Sunday for it to only return the next weekend. All I could do was grab the paper book of Oraciones with the rosary on the front cover, standing in front of the cross that was lying on top of a dresser next to the wooden paneled wall whispering in repetition El Padre Nuestro, Dios te salve María, y la Gloria. I thought the more times I prayed the faster the drinking would stop, and the faster family would say goodbye for the night. I was so desperate to feel safe again that I would return to my room to pray throughout the family gatherings and build up enough courage to walk back out and help light up cigarettes, empty out ashtrays, and replace the empty beer bottles.

I could easily tell when my parents were past the buzz stage and intoxicated—slurred speech, bloodshot eyes, and unable to walk straight. Maybe that's the reason why my observation skills are extra heightened. I would look for the signs to take myself out of the room before a fight broke out, which it did many times. The arguments and fights were guaranteed to happen when you mixed alcohol and a strong personality like my mother's. Mi mami decia "yo no me dejo de nadie." She enjoyed confrontations and would let it be known that she was not a person who would surrender. She was what Colombians call a berraca. She was badass.

One Saturday night, a fight broke out in our front yard—my mother lunged at my dad and scratched his face. I ran towards them thinking I could stop the fight. All I could do was grab my dad's hand and pull him as hard as a little girl could crying and scared saying Papi todo esta bien, por favor Papi—por favor Papi vamos adentro. I kept repeating this trying to withhold my feelings as I normally did. For a hot minute and probably for the first time my dad saw the fear in my eyes and my voice and he listened. My sister and family held my mother back, and I could see my mom's eyes bulging wide open and yelling at the top of her lungs. It was a scary scene for my little eyes to watch.Something happened, the moment my father listened to me telling him "Everything is okay, Papi"—we held hands and walked back into the house. He sat on my bed, and I sat next to him. I tried to be brave and not let him or anyone see my fear and anxiety, but that night he saw me with all of my tangled emotions. I was able to finally cry without being told—por que llora? Quiere que le de razón para llorar. When my mother would tell me that I would instantly make myself stop crying, not easy to do, but the alternative was worse. My dad was visibly angry about what had happened, and his pride wouldn't let him apologize. Nonetheless, I felt heard.

At the end of these family gatherings, my sister and I would turn into caretakers. My sister's job was to help my mother off the floor and get her to bed next to my father who was already snoring. My job was to get the bright green laundry basket. You might be thinking that's weird. Well, the laundry basket was multi-purpose— most things growing up had more than one use given the lack of money. In this case, the laundry basket was also the pail with handles where my mother's head would disappear after drinking. The end of the night would be marked by the clean-up work that was left for us. Honestly, I preferred picking up the cases of beer in the kitchen and living room and cleaning out the ashtrays instead of seeing my mother drunk. I felt awful watching her.

Slowly, the weekend gatherings became less frequent, the cases of beer were fewer, and less family would come to visit. Things seemed to be shifting for the better or so I thought until suddenly, my parents told us we weren't going to live together anymore. Anxiety and fear settled back in with comfort this time around. In my young little mind, I didn't see this coming. There was no explanation provided other than the decision was made. I was going to live with my mother and sister and that was it.

The divorce was yet another painful experience because I loved my dad and didn't want this for my family. I was afraid of my mother and my dad made me feel safe other than when he was drinking. I couldn't question why they didn't ask me how I felt because it wouldn't have mattered. This time it was the loss of being a family that drove my emotions because you see my dad and I spent a lot of quality time together. We raked the leaves in the Fall, shoveled snow in the Winter, cut the grass in the Summer—we were always doing something together. He attended my parent-teacher conferences and with his broken English tried his best to communicate with the teacher. We would walk out of the classroom holding hands with a smile on our faces.

Those were the moments I knew I had made him proud. He took an interest in the things that I cared about such as school and playing catch or going to the park. We did what all families would do, and not living together as a family broke my heart. I remember crying from my gut, alone in my room to the point where my forehead was blotchy, and my eyes hurt because they were so swollen from the emotional pain I was feeling inside. There was only one thing to do—pray. "Dios por favor ayuda a mi familia para que no se separen." Please help keep my family together.

Soon, it was just the three of us again. My mother spent a lot of time in bed feeling unwell and uninterested. Looking back now, my mother was in a deep depression. I don't know if she realized she was depressed. Heck, I don't think anyone in our family noticed either, and if they did they weren't going to mention it to her because it would be met with deflection and end in an argument. At this point, Pat had graduated high school and immediately began working for the U.S. Postal Service in order to cover the expenses since we were back in an apartment and my mom was in and out of jobs.

Everything felt weird without my dad. Now the only way to connect was via phone calls and short visits in his car. He didn't come inside the apartment to avoid arguing. I don't know whose idea it was to get divorced, but my dad was moving forward with his single life again and my mother struggled. Depression and anger took the driver's seat, and she began to say mean things about my dad to get me to stop talking to him. She would listen in on my conversations with him and ask me questions after every visit. She wanted to know what was going on in his life. I was 12 years old and in the middle of this crazy relationship. I didn't want to displease anyone, so I tried to keep conversations about my visits with my dad short. Knowing what to say and what not to say was important. If I said something that bothered her, then I would have to answer more questions.

My mom never cried over her divorce, come to think of it I've never seen my mom get a good cry for anything or anyone. I guess she's tough as a rock, but it was evident that she was regretting the divorce. This went on through my high school years, and I just kept shoving down the anger and resentment I felt for being put in the middle of this hell. I ignored the invasion of privacy although I knew it wasn't right and certainly not fair that I was being manipulated. I told myself that if I ever got divorced, I would never put my kids through this. Getting grilled by my mother after every visit or phone call was filled with anxiety and stress.

Yet, I still dreamed that one day my parents would reunite, and we would be a family again. How could I possibly be thinking that was a good idea? Clearly, I was willing to deal with the arguments as long as my family was together. As a junior in high school, something clicked for me because I took all of my anxiety and put it to good use by pouring myself into schoolwork. It paid off because I was on my way to college ready to pursue a degree in Accounting. The excitement of getting away and not being in the middle of my parents' ongoing mess was exactly what I wanted but didn't really know how to do as a teenager. The desire to get away from my mother led me to focus on what really mattered to me—my future. It had to look and feel different from what my mother's life was like. I loaded up my day with classes and two jobs. I enjoyed learning and this was my ticket to peace and quiet.

As a Latina, working hard was expected and it never mattered what the job was as long as you were learning skills. School and work were in NYC, so riding the bus and subway became my new way of life. The hustle and bustle of NYC was attractive to me. Everyone dressed in their business suits and sneakers with their newspaper in hand sparked a new desire—I wanted to become a successful businesswoman, who wore a business suit and heels to the office.

My vision was very clear. I was going to live the life I was meant to live, the one I would design and plan, the one that would break through generational chains of scarcity, distrust, greed, narcissism, and addiction. Escaping the life that my parents had to live because of limitations that were generationally fueled with adversity and struggle to a life where all my needs were met—a successful career where I could impact others' lives, a loving spouse who had my back no matter what, and children whom I would provide a better upbringing to than my own. I was determined to achieve this life and worked hard to do exactly that.

While in college I began working in my chosen career and had a mentor for the first time in my life. Yvette was a Latina who took an interest in things that mattered to me. She would ask about my classes and how work was going. Honestly, I always starved for attention from my mother. How was it that a total stranger was more interested in me than my mother? Whether true or not, that was my perception. Work offered me the best escape from my living nightmare. My schedule had me out of the house from 6:30 am to 10 pm. There was no time for arguments because, by the time I got home, my mother was ready to go to sleep.

Of course, I never gave up on trying to have a conversation with her that involved sharing about my day. However, she would change the subject to talk about her day. I couldn't understand why she wasn't interested in hearing about what I was up to in school or work.Luckily, I was blessed with great role models. My sister Pat was my very first role model and my earth angel. Pat is ten years older than me, and we both lived through my story together, and in many ways, she lived through a lot more painful experiences than I did. Her sense of humor was undeniably the love medicine I needed. She would look into my eyes, and I would ask what do you see—she responded "John Travolta." I believed John Travolta's picture was in my eyes. Hahaha --John Travolta in my eyes. I did have a crush on him just like so many others after watching him in Saturday Night Fever. These small interactions made me smile and I'm pretty sure I blushed at knowing that John was in my eyes.

My sister protected me from the hard discipline my mother led with, so much so that my mother earned the name Mohammad Ali, a boxing champion. Pat found laughter in everything good or bad. We have memories where we were laughing so hard that I would literally have to run to the bathroom because my bladder couldn't handle it. It was that non-stop giggly laugh that brought tears to my eyes while hugging my stomach because it hurt in a good way from how hard we were laughing. God blessed my sister in many ways, but her humor is like no other, and she was the best medicine for me and for others. My earth angel was sent with a purpose to bring joy, and happiness and celebrate the good.

Throughout our lives, we are blessed with earth angels who serve a very important purpose in our life, and some have come and gone – I'm truly blessed that my sister Pat has been the most special angel and I'm so grateful to have lived through some of the most painful times of my life with her by my side. Pat lifted my spirits with her infectious humor, she showed me that embracing change was for the better and that we didn't have to be stuck in old ways of thinking the way my mother was.

This is how Latinas rise and transform through different seasons of life. We lean on our hermandad, the sisterhood of family, friends, earth angels, sponsors, and mentors to drop seeds of inspiration, confidence, perspective and possibilities in our souls. All it takes is one seed to take root and with the right nurturing an aspiration for a brighter future grows. We are gracious because we learn to embrace what comes to us and what leaves us without questioning it. We work through the challenges and find the small and big successes to share with others. We are badasses known for our exceptional resilience, our strong optimism, and putting others' needs before our own—we are a force in society y no nos dejamos por vencidas. We do not give up, we try harder, we dream bigger, and we believe in ourselves and in the new generations of Latinas to come. We pay homage to the scars earned from lessons learned and change so that something new can be born. We've raised our conscious awareness and vibrational energy to break those generational chains that have overstayed their welcome.

I am fortunate to have been blessed with two daughters who are both inspirational leaders of their own paths in life. While their lives are not free from struggles, they are certainly free from the chains that I carried at their age. My hope is that they and the new generation of Latinas berracas will continue to pave new roads in creating an equal level playing field for all. From one badass Latina to another—trust your inner voice, use it loudly and embrace everything that happens to you and I mean everything for it is a gift that will transform your life into the life you are meant to live.

ABOUT MARIA MOLINA MONROY

Maria Molina Monroy is a first-generation Colombian-American and first-time author. She hopes to inspire new generations of Latinas to transform their lives into the life they are meant to live. She was born and raised in the diverse melting pot of Queens, New York where she survived her parents' tumultuous relationship, and immersed herself into a future of breaking free from generational chains. After graduating from Baruch College-CUNY, Maria built a successful career in Human Resources Management that spanned three decades. She is an advocate and ally for women and underrepresented minorities highlighting the importance of mentors and sponsors. Maria is currently prioritizing her self-care through art, meditation, yoga, and exercise. You can find Maria in her happy place dancing to Latin music, even though she may occasionally be off-beat clapping and snapping her fingers. She enjoys family trips, family movies, and dining in new restaurants. She now lives in Los Angeles, CA with her husband Rob, and three kids—Sofia, Tanya, and Mateo and two pet friends Benito and Luna.

Email: mmmbfly@gmail.com

6
MARIE CAMACHO

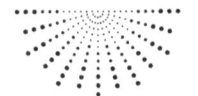

THE WEIGHT OF SILENCE

*A*fter our workout, the ladies from the Livestrong program and I made our way to the locker room. As we changed, each one of us opened up about the challenges we faced after overcoming cancer. One woman spoke of her struggles with a sick spouse, while another shared the difficulties of living alone. I felt their joy as we told our stories, but also their sadness when it was time to part ways. Each goodbye echoed with the weight of unspoken burdens, a reminder of the loneliness that often accompanied our shared journey.

Despite the well-meaning words of encouragement from others urging us to "be positive" and "be grateful," it was clear that these sentiments only served to deepen our sense of isolation. As a Latina woman, raised in a culture where emotions were often overlooked and vulnerability was seen as weakness, I understood their struggle all too well.

Growing up in The Bronx, I was the ultimate Nuyorican music enthusiast, dreaming of hitting the big stage as a singer. Cheez Whiz, Wonder Bread, and music videos were my daily fuel. As a little dreamer, I dodged the chaos of reality by mentally jetting off to the cheerful worlds I saw on TV.

Back then, kids were expected to be silent ninjas—seen but not heard. Wearing a white dress was a high-stakes game of "keep it spotless," and if someone offered you cookies, you had to turn them down; accepting food of any kind meant people would think your folks were not feeding you at home. Like many young Latinas, I mastered the art of creating a picture of perfection. Anything outside of that brought huge embarrassment and shame to the family.

If trouble found you, somehow it was your fault. Complaining was a one-way ticket to being labeled weak, a mood killer, or just plain hypersensitive. Dreams, those glittery orbs of ambition, were dismissed as mere bubbles: delicate, fleeting, and easily popped. This was all a tough pill to swallow for someone who daydreamed of being the next Gloria Estefan, grooving through life with infectious music and happiness.

Anything heavy—problems, trauma, or the awkward stuff—never got discussed. Your choices were to keep it moving or confess your secrets to the church walls.

~

Both my parents were born and raised in Patillas, Puerto Rico. My father epitomized the essence of hard work. In New York, he juggled two demanding jobs. With tireless dedication, he managed to purchase our Arthur Avenue home outright for $9,000. His achievements were remarkable, especially considering the hurdles he faced. My admiration for his ambition knew no bounds. However, his communication style with us left much to be desired and whenever feelings of sadness or stress arose for him, they were frequently drowned in a bottle of Bacardi rum.

In the same household, my mother's presence brought a contrasting energy of warmth and creativity, though tinged with unspoken struggles. The kitchen, her realm, was always alive with the sounds of boleros or trios from the WAPA radio, combined with the eagerly anticipated horoscopes of Walter Mercado. Her love for games, crocheting, and sewing brought moments of joy and artistry into our daily lives. Yet, beneath her vibrant interests and the love she showered on us, my mother battled silent foes—low self-esteem, depression, and social anxiety. These unseen challenges confined her to the home, a stark contrast to the lively streets of The Bronx, so different from what she was accustomed to in La Isla del Encanto.

∼

Picture this: a headband as my royal crown, a laundry line playing the part of my golden lasso, and bracelets made from good ol' painter's tape. Oh, and let's not forget the superhero-friendly plastic-covered furniture trend of the time—a real boon for a fledgling heroine like me.

Every leap onto the sofa would produce a swooshing sound, my personal soundtrack to accompany me as I soared through the air and zipped around like the Flash. "Deja de brincar en el sofa!" my mom's voice would echo from the kitchen. Ignoring her warning, I faced her entrance, chancla in hand, ready for battle. But fear? Nah, I blocked every swing with my trusty masking tape bracelets.

As the chaos unfolded, my mom, slowly grasping the absurdity of it all, couldn't contain her laughter. And there I stood, Wonder Woman-style, feeling like I had accomplished a superhero mission. It was that wild and vivid imagination that saw me through the highs and lows of childhood, turning everyday moments into epic adventures.

Despite my desire for action, from the moment I arrived in this world, a set of gender expectations were waiting for me, like an unwelcome party I never RSVP'd to. For instance, girls are expected to speak only when spoken to and not dominate the conversation. You're supposed to be friendly, but not so friendly that you seem flirtatious. Confidence is encouraged, but too much can be seen as intimidating, especially to men. Making sound decisions is important, yet every choice is scrutinized. There's pressure to aim higher, but not too high, as it can be perceived negatively. Standing up for yourself is applauded, yet it often leads to blame and questions about what you did to cause the situation. Keeping up with these expectations was exhausting. The list seemed endless and utterly draining for my younger self.

As the years passed and I entered adulthood, I quickly learned that the mixed messages and expectations of conformity I had experienced weren't relegated to childhood. Almost overnight, everyone around me seemed fixated on marriage and parenthood, and I couldn't stand it. It troubled me how these aspirations overshadowed everything else they desired or dreamed of. I yearned to be different, to explore the world, embark on new adventures, and break out of who I was expected to be. By the age of 25, I was happily unmarried and relishing every moment of independence. However, my dad didn't share my enthusiasm. "Hija, apurate porque se te va ir el tren," he once urged. Despite his efforts for so many years to shield me from dating and unplanned pregnancies, suddenly, I felt pressured. How disheartening. I wonder if he would've felt the same if I were a son? If I had to bet, I'd say probably not.

In my thirties, my commitment-phobic self did a complete 180 once I met my now-husband José. Suddenly, I understood what all my friends had been talking about in my twenties, and I was pumped for this new chapter. When we got engaged I rang up my dad pronto. Turns out, José had beaten me to it and already had "the talk" with him about marrying yours truly. That tickled me pink, especially since it checked off a box on the "expected behavior" list. I figured

Dad would be over the moon, so I spilled all our plans about tying the knot the following year. But instead of joining me in my excitement, he hit me with, "You're lucky that at your age someone asked you; Casate rapído." Cue the train metaphor again! This locomotive of doom just kept chugging along behind me. I couldn't shake it off, and it irked me to no end. And just when I thought Dad was the only engineer on board, after I got married, suddenly everyone was fretting about it leaving the station. Now, the focus was on baby-making.

∼

As I held baby G in my arms, I wondered how it was possible to love someone you just met so much. She had the prettiest pouty lips, cheekbones like her dad, and the longest lashes I had ever seen. Our little girl was so precious, but we needed to say goodbye. Our hearts broke into a million pieces, José and I both gave her a kiss on her forehead and with a heavy heart handed her over to the nurse.

José stayed with me that night. We laid in silence just holding each other on the hospital bed, each hoping that this was all a bad nightmare. Yet the physical and emotional pain from the delivery was sharp enough to convince us both of the cruel reality of what we just experienced.

Hours earlier, my water had broken. I was just a little over 20 weeks pregnant. After telling me everything was going to be OK, the doctor came back in to inform us that I had lost too much amniotic fluid and that there wasn't enough for the baby to survive or develop without complications. The decision that she was insinuating for José and me to make made our hearts scream in pain. Just a few minutes ago our baby was on the monitor almost waving at us, and now this? We prayed for God to help us know what to do. Then, before we could make a final decision, I broke out in a fever, indicating the onset of an infection. The decision had been made for us: The pregnancy had to be terminated.

Just like that, Baby G was gone.

∼

In the morning, still in shock, we packed my stuff. On the cab ride home, once again, silence accompanied us. When we arrived at our building, we walked quickly past the doorman and into the elevator. As the doors were about to close, someone cried out "Hold the elevator." José held the door and, quickly, a man rushed in, followed by a woman. She was visibly pregnant. "Thank you," said the man, standing close to the woman who, judging by the ring on her hand, was his wife. His palm rested gently on her belly, and they both radiated pure happiness.

In the opposite corner, I stood, watching them and clutching onto José as if he were my lifeline. It felt as though a sharp knife was twisting deeper into my heart with each passing breath I struggled to take. In that poignant moment, the harsh reality of life's cruelty and unfairness hit me. Questions swirled like a storm in my mind, each one more piercing than the last, as I wondered what I had done to deserve such unbearable pain. I surely caused this, right? The weight of that belief gnawed at my soul, leaving me utterly devastated and bewildered.

As the days passed and the pain of losing Baby G overwhelmed me, I found myself receiving numerous messages from those around me, both explicit and implied, dictating how I should cope with the tragedy that had befallen me. There was an unmistakable pressure to swiftly move on from my grief, coupled with warnings about how lingering in devastation would greatly affect my relationship with my husband. "Vaz estar bien. Muchas mujeres pasan por eso. Tu esposo should never see you like this. Just focus on trying again" they would say. I was expected to put on a brave face and quickly overcome the most profound heartbreak I had ever endured. Yet, once again I couldn't help but wonder: if I were a man, would I be given the same advice? Was José also being instructed to suppress his emotions to preserve our relationship? Somehow, I doubted it.

The following months buzzed with family and friend celebrations—weddings, baptisms, baby welcomings—each one requesting our presence. Surrounded by laughter and love, I buried my emotions deep within, refusing to cast a shadow over my husband and those around me, trying hard to follow the advice of putting on a brave face. Yet, inside, I felt like I was slowly suffocating, drowning in a whirlpool of grief. Nevertheless, I pushed forward, projecting an image of strength, and convincing myself and others that the pain was already behind me.

When asked how I was feeling, I typically mustered a cheerful response, swiftly diverting the conversation to lighter topics. One evening, with a drink giving me courage (I am such a lightweight), I took a risk among a group of women I felt close to. When they posed the same question, I couldn't hold back. The words spilled out, revealing the raw ache in my heart. Noticing the shock on their faces, I felt like I had broken some code or pact I'd never agreed to. One of them even whispered, "Wow, I didn't expect all that." I found myself shutting down and wishing I had simply painted the picture of perfection that I was raised to portray.

∼

After much thought and consideration, José and I made the decision to start anew by purchasing a house and relocating to Stamford, CT. There, we continued our efforts to expand our family, undergoing the highs and lows of numerous unsuccessful IVF attempts and miscarriages. As each setback wore away at our hopes, doubts started creeping in, casting shadows on our dreams of echoing laughter in the hallways of our home.

When I dared to express these concerns, I was once again reminded by family members of the strain it could place on my marriage. "No le digas nada a José. Ningun Hombre wants to hear that. And you don't want him seeking elsewhere for what you can't provide."

Haunted by that notion, though it angered me, I feared that what they were advising could be true, and I buried my feelings deep within, concealing them from sight. As the unspoken weight of fears pressed down on me, I felt myself slipping into the depths of despair. But in those darkest moments, I sought refuge in prayer, pouring out my soul in heartfelt pleas. I wrestled with the agony of losing our baby girl, yearning for signs, for answers to the relentless questions of why and what role I played in our tragedy.

With no response in sight, I demanded clarity, even issuing a defiant ultimatum: "If I don't conceive before 40, then so be it. I don't want any kids." And, in a twist of fate as unexpected as it was miraculous, that very year, on the cusp of turning 40, divine intervention answered my plea.

José and I were blessed with not one, but two precious gifts: a radiant baby girl, welcomed into our lives through the miracle of adoption, and a strapping baby boy, conceived naturally, defying all odds and bypassing the need for IVF. Amid tears of joy and disbelief, we realized that sometimes, the most extraordinary blessings arrive on God's *"train"* schedule and no one else's.

∽

In the warm embrace of August 2015, we celebrated our son's 2nd birthday. We love hosting and getting our family and friends together, and what better occasion than to celebrate one of our little ones? That evening, after the birthday candles were blown out and the chaos subsided, we lovingly bathed our babies, read them bedtime stories, and tucked them in. As I watched them sleeping peacefully, a profound sense of tranquility and love filled my heart. I couldn't believe this was *my* family—something that, for a long time, I never thought would be possible. As José and I nestled in bed together that night going over the day's events, we were both so very happy. "I can't believe that we are finally going to have a calm year. One with no drama. It feels incredible," I said to him before turning out the light. We hugged, the next unknown hurdle lingering in the stillness.

∼

The promised tranquility of that summer day swiftly unraveled with the arrival of September. I had dismissed the sensitive feeling in my breasts for the past few months as a mere side effect of my monthly cycle. However, when the sensitivity persisted, a sense of unease began to creep in. A self-exam in the shower revealed a lump. Seeking solace and confirmation, I turned to José, who acknowledged its presence. "It's probably nothing, but for your peace of mind, get it checked," he advised. The following day, an appointment was scheduled, leading to a cascade of tests after the ominous mammogram results.

Then came September 29th, a day that would alter the course of my life and that of my loved ones. The nurse from the Tully Center left a voicemail, initiating a day of missed connections. When we finally spoke, her words hit me like a freight train: "You have cancer." In that moment, with my babies napping and José away on business, the world around me fell into a haunting silence. Her words continued, outlining the urgency of the steps that needed to be taken. Numb with shock, I mechanically murmured my consent, the gravity of the situation eluding full comprehension.

Following that initial call, everything felt like a whirlwind at 100 mph. My mind was swirling with the influx of information coming my way. José immediately began reaching out to every friend who could help us find the best doctor possible. Our days became consumed with a flurry of appointments and finding someone who could possibly find a mistake in my diagnosis. Yet, despite seeing four different oncologists, all affiliated with prestigious hospitals, the consensus was alarming and consistent. The cancer was moving fast, and chemotherapy wasn't just an option but an absolute necessity. The situation was incredibly bewildering and frightening. How was it possible that nine months before this diagnosis my mammogram showed nothing and now the cancer was moving rapidly? It didn't make sense, and I feared what it all would mean for my little ones.

Once we had a plan in place, José and I decided to share the news with our family and friends. Our children's preschool rallied around us, and our extended family offered immense support. We felt held. However, my body was another story—it completely shut down on chemo. I developed a painful fissure that led to an infection, and with my white blood cell count dropping to zero, I was quarantined for ten agonizing days. During that time, my faith wavered, and I truly thought I might not survive. I cried not just for myself, but for my babies, who I had fought so hard to have.

Because my body was reacting so poorly to the treatment, it was decided to cut it short. Originally scheduled for 18 rounds, I ended at 14. After enduring chemo, a series of surgeries, and hormone replacement therapy, everyone was ready for my body to begin healing and so was I. But emotionally, I was in turmoil. The cocktail of Lupron and Letrozole wreaked havoc on my physical and mental well-being, and the disappointing outcome of my first reconstruction surgery only added to my distress.

Amidst the support, I once again found myself burdened by the weight of the cultural expectations that had trailed me since childhood. "Ya estás bien hija. You're all clear now. Your family needs you. Dale Gracias a Dios and move forward," they said. The concern over how my husband would perceive me loomed larger than my own feelings. The roles of wife and mother were thrust upon me, with no room for a gradual return to myself. It felt as if I was expected to bounce back as if from a vacation, leaving the kids with my husband while I played the role of the "bad selfish wife"... but wait, hadn't I endured 14 rounds of grueling chemotherapy and double mastectomy? Why did it seem like he was the one who had faced the toughest ordeal? Expressing my emotions seemed futile, for it not only affected those around me but also served no purpose. Surviving was paramount. My breast being butchered during reconstruction, the neuropathy in my hands and feet from chemo, the premature hot flashes and joint pains, the complete loss of desire for intimacy—all of it was to be buried in silence.

For his part, my husband never demanded perfection or stifled my vulnerability; in fact, he encouraged it. Yet, despite his understanding, I harbored resentment towards him. I resented that he did not deal with the pressures I did. How if the tables had been turned he wouldn't have been expected to jump right into his prescribed gender role. How through every tragic moment in our lives everyone seemed more concerned about how "MY" struggles affected him. And how I was constantly reminded of his needs and if not met it was only natural for him to stray.

To speak of any of my heartache and struggle was to be labeled a downer, ungrateful for the second chance at life that I had been given, and the wonderful husband who after everything he had to endure, didn't cheat on me.

∽

"So, Marie, how are you feeling?" inquired a close friend, their voice laced with concern. Every time they reached out, I sensed a longing to confide, but past experiences of being abruptly cut off stifled my willingness to open up fully. In hopes that it would be different this time around, I decided to share my struggles.

"Actually, I've been in so much pain, and it's been really hard for me to walk because of my..." I began, only to be swiftly interrupted.

"But the good thing is that you are now on the other side. So, you're good," my friend interjected, their words washing over me like a dismissive wave.

In that instant, fury consumed me. "Why bother asking how I am feeling if you're only going to silence me?" I demanded, my voice edged with frustration. "If you already know the answer you want to hear, then spare me and just answer it for me. Why does everyone want me to be OK? I'm not OK and if I can't be honest with you about my emotions, whether good or bad, then perhaps it's better you don't call at all."

With all the suppressed rage of years being stifled by others, I abruptly ended the call. I knew I had wounded my friend, but in that moment, it felt cathartic to release the floodgates of truth. Tears poured down my face like a torrential rainstorm, my cries echoing in our shower bathroom. I had reached my breaking point. No more carefully crafting my words to hide the raw truth of my emotions. No more shielding my marriage by pretending everything was fine when it wasn't. Admitting that I was not okay, admitting that I was battling depression—damn it, if that was going to be the final straw, then so be it. After all we had gone through, I refused to carry the weight of silence any longer.

That one conversation was a wake-up call, revealing the load of emotions I had been harboring inside. To this day, I can't understand: Why does sharing my truth make so many so uncomfortable? Facing the relentless pressures of aging and struggling with infertility is incredibly difficult. Delivering a baby only to have to say goodbye is heart-wrenching and tragic. Getting diagnosed with cancer just when you felt like you were finally able to come up for air f—ing sucks. All of these experiences *sucked*! And not being OK because of it, is and should be OK. Opening up about the full range of our experiences is what makes us human, not weak or a bad wife, mother, or friend.

Embracing these truths helped me realize how all my life I had pushed aside what was important to me and who I truly was, all for the sake of others' comfort and the expectations put on me starting from a young age.

I've lost touch with the Livestrong ladies from the locker room. It's been approximately seven years since we've seen each other. Yet, their memory lingers in my heart, and I often find myself wondering how they are doing as I reflect on our shared paths.

As for me, I've become an open book, sharing my journey with anyone willing to listen, even if it means *oversharing* at times and possibly losing a friend or two. I also founded One Tough Cookie, a nonprofit that supports those dealing with cancer and the intense emotions that accompany it.

Life hasn't been easy, but through it I've learned that true support means standing beside someone, holding their hand, and committing to ride with them on whatever "train" comes their way, no matter how uncomfortable it gets.

ABOUT MARIE CAMACHO

Marie L. Camacho is the founder of One Tough Cookie, a nonprofit organization dedicated to uplifting those dealing with cancer. As a cancer survivor herself, Marie is passionate about paying forward the support she received during her own journey. Her personal experience fuels her mission to provide encouragement and hope to others facing similar challenges.

Beyond her work with One Tough Cookie, Marie has always dreamt of being a singer and harbors hopes of one day performing for Gloria Estefan. She is also an avid writer and a powerful voice for those who resonate with her story, using her platform to inspire and connect with others.

Marie cherishes family gatherings and enjoys spending quality time with her loved ones. She often goes on hikes and road trips with her husband, José, and their children, Adán and Tahlia. Accompanying them on these adventures is their adorable mini poodle, Thor, who adds an extra dose of joy to their lives.

Marie Camacho's dedication to her nonprofit, combined with her artistic aspirations and love for her family, paints a picture of a multifaceted woman committed to making a positive impact in the world.

Website: *www.supportonetoughcookie.com*
Facebook: *www.facebook.com/supportonetoughcookie*
Instagram: *www.instagram.com/supportonetoughcookie*

7
ANNETT VELASQUEZ

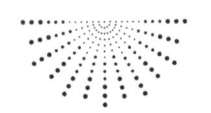

***L*ife happens for you, not to you. Until you understand that, you'll be in your own way.**

Community has always been present in my life beginning within my family. Recently, the importance of valuing community was intensely solidified in my personal experience. As a first-generation Mexican American woman, I've discovered how my experiences and environment caused conflicting realizations regarding my self-awareness (Libra rising in the house!). Awareness, to me, is having a healthy mindset, diet, morals, beliefs, and lifestyle. However, not everyone is self-aware of how our unresolved emotions and stress can affect each aspect previously mentioned.

Consequently, I value health as it is crucial in our daily lives. I learned health encompasses mental, emotional, and physical well-being after I gave birth to my son. I struggled to feel like "myself" after the delivery and didn't realize I had post-partum depression (PPD). PPD wasn't discussed due to my family's inability to be in tune with their own feelings paired with their resistance to freely express any unpleasant feelings. It wasn't until my post-partum depression subsided that I was able to recognize the importance of prioritizing my own health. That was the moment I started intentionally implementing a well-balanced diet, stable emotional environment, and reciprocal relationships that contributed to my well-being. If I hadn't purposefully created healthy relationships with my family and friends, I probably would have been depressed for longer than 2 years.

Essentially, my support system helped me get through a very difficult time and my gratitude for them is endless. My Mexican heritage upholds traditional values that uphold patriarchal norms and imply self-abandoning as a woman. These cultural norms remain in the subconscious and create limiting mindsets. In my experience, people-pleasing tendencies were at the forefront of my family values, especially with the elderly and authoritative figures. This value system also caused a sense of unity since, from a young age, I contributed to the wellness of others. I have always enjoyed contributing to the wellness of others.

However, it took me decades to understand that I needed to have limits and boundaries and even refuse to be *acomedida* (attentive). One of my coaches, Michelle Gomez, once shared that "sometimes we have to be a bad daughter, to be good to ourselves." That opened many mental doors for me. A large family is normal in Mexican culture, especially since I came from an immigrant family. My grandfather came over to the States as a Bracero during the 50's due to a worker shortage from WW II. He decided to officially leave Mexico and moved to the U.S. in 1977. He would slowly move the rest of the family which included my grandmother, 7 tias (which doesn't include my mom), and my uncle. My youngest aunt was the only US-born child. She was born in Texas, and she is a Cancer. She is our family's glue. She is always in support of her sisters, friends or anyone she can lend a helping hand to. Cancer women are believed to be a true embodiment of nurturance and unconditional love and support, to name a few characteristics.

My family arrived in Huntington Park in the late 1970's. My grandfather brought the three eldest children with him to establish themselves financially, first. My grandmother and the three youngest daughters followed thereafter. Lastly, the three middle children, which included my mother, and 2 other aunts, were the last to migrate. Logistically, their migration waves made sense, however, I feel that this had lasting emotional impacts on them all. Specifically, 3 of them suffer from mental health problems. I strongly believe that what isn't expressed, will manifest in a disorder or ailment (check out Dr. Joe Dispenza or Gabor Mate if this interests you).

Fast forward, years later, my uncle ended up purchasing a home in Watts, CA in 1987. He was able to focus on his personal goals as typically males in the family do. Men are not held back by familial responsibilities like women are. When my mom became pregnant with my younger brother, my parents moved my older sister and me away from the family when I was 5 years old, to Inglewood, CA where I began preschool at Centinela Park. My mom worked a lot, and my father spent a large portion of my youth intermittently incarcerated. I spent a lot of time with my maternal family since they were a huge support system for my siblings and me. My assigned identity as the peacemaker in many family dynamics allowed others to treat me with little consideration, kind of the way a gateway city is an open road. I unintentionally helped bridge the gap between Aunts who didn't (or couldn't) cook, my actions ensured we had the next meal ready for everyone.

On the bright side, I did learn my way around the kitchen, so for that I am grateful. I dislike engaging in drama in general, so I didn't mind being the neutralizer of certain domestic situations. If it meant I would be the butt of a joke to ease tension, that would be better than to feel the tension. If it meant I had to help with tamales because other relatives couldn't or didn't want to, I stepped up, no questions asked. Since I was unable to voice my frustrations, I internalized the belief that what I had to say didn't matter, along with my feelings. I lived with this narrative in my mind for years.

"It is written in the stars" and I don't say that lightly. I am a firm believer in astrology (in case you hadn't noticed) and have recently started exploring how my birth chart has shaped the woman I have become and aspire to be. I understand your chart won't give you all the answers, but information will arrive at different moments, if you are open to receiving them. I have known for some time that I was made for great achievements. Growing up I recall the words of my first-grade teacher, Ms. Herndon, saying "You're going to be somebody one day". She knew then, I would grow up to make a difference in the world. The unknown is always scary, partly because we know that as much as we plan, things may not pan out as we plan.

Trusting that things will work out in the best way possible is a surefire way to remain calm and present. After all, that's what all of this is about, God's gift (presence). Remembering that things happen for us no matter how hard it is, is the deepest form of surrender in my opinion. Trust is a divine feminine trait that requires us to have faith. This is our feminine essence we all must embody in a healthy balance with our masculine energy (doing). As a Libra rising, part of my journey is about finding balance in all aspects of my life. This has been challenging as a Capricorn (January birth month), whose value was deemed on being structured, organized, and productive. Most of my life was lived in extremes because I didn't embrace the grey area due to a lack of safety physically, mentally, and emotionally. Fortunately, both of my parents have always been spiritual and believed in the divine and things always working out, no matter how hard life gets. As a middle child, finding my voice was always challenging, but as I became a mother at 22 years of age, I had to start somewhere. Whether it was explaining my reasoning for my parenting choices or asking for support with caring for my child, I could no longer hide in the shadows of my childhood shame.

The same way you don't value that passageway (avenue or boulevard) until it's inaccessible or closed (or in my case upset or unwilling), is how I felt during my adolescence now that I have looked back objectively. One of my favorite true gateways is Atlantic Blvd as it connects two neighboring cities, which led us to authentic restaurants as I was a student worker at East Los Angeles College

(ELAC). I share that because there are so many gateways all around LA and just like I have felt, I'm sure there are so many others too. There's hardly any traffic (or resistance in my case) on that stretch, and it's a smooth ride (IYKYK).

Metaphorically, the easiest method of self-abandonment I embodied was people pleasing, even if it meant costing my self-esteem. I remember dissociating as early as 8 years old (due to SA by a close family member). Because children are so resilient, they adjust to most situations to maintain their sanity, without even knowing it. My family dynamic was very misconstrued since I was a child internalizing everything that happened around me as "normal." We all tend to do this. It felt normal to take orders and not question anything. I partly blame my Capricorn sun for respecting order and structure presented by authority as the law of the land, which was why I didn't question it. As you mature and grow older, you realize a lot of stories in your head are just that. As humans, we intellectualize pain to make it bearable, I know that's what I did. Intellectualizing the pain helps make it more bearable and empathize with the "reason" as to why you are in a particular circumstance. You may even start to realize how you've maintained yourself in certain roles, based on your made-up stories. This is known as the "victim" mentality which takes some time to accept and heal.

The American ideology is very selfish because "self" comes before anyone, or anything else. There is no consideration of others since lack and greed are prominent in this society. Through my studies, I have come to realize that both cultures (Mexican and American), require a delicate balance that is personalized to everyone who can relate to those labels. Most extremes can be harmful, yet many of us grew up with black-and-white thinking to create a sense of control. It was a survival tool, that I have come to realize, is no longer necessary. I am trusting and finding beauty in the grey area since that's where magic can happen. Allowing people & things to come and go is also crucial during these moments.

I was reminded of the importance of community on my recent

trip to Teotihuacan (known for being "where the Gods were created"). The temples all have significant alignment with many astrological occurrences. The smell of wet dirt and the astounding magnitude of the pyramids displayed a deep sense of communal gatherings being a central focus of this society. They were not consumed by capitalism or instant gratification. They were in true alignment with the cosmos, and life for that matter. They prioritized their family and thereby the greater good of all. Having 7 aunts (on my maternal side) allowed me to receive love and support in ways, I felt, my parents were unable to. When I say community, I am referencing my experience of family dynamics.

Back to my time at East L.A. College, I remember thinking "Once I can take the 10 Westbound for home, I know I've made it." I'd associated a particular side of town with success. I remember even feeling the air quality difference when I was in East L.A. versus my hometown, Inglewood. It was at minimum a 10-degree difference on a hot summer day between those two cities. What I have recently discovered is that the further we go into areas where there are underrepresented communities, the higher the prevalence of environmental racism.

There is a tool called CalEnviroscreen where you can track various environmental exposures, and it is very clear that lower-income communities are suffering a greater inequity when compared to affluent neighborhoods. To be more specific, particulate matter (PM), is higher on the East side of town when compared to the West side. PM are small particles that can move into the lungs when we breathe and some have been shown to cause adverse health effects like heart & lung diseases. Some populations are more vulnerable to this which include the elderly, children, and those suffering from a chronic illness. Systemic racism is one of the many reasons why I went into Public Health, and I am very passionate about informing others to minimize poor health outcomes in my community.

Since becoming a mother, I realized a lot. Just before having my son, I was introduced to Public Health while I was attending a transfer fair at ELAC, and I immediately began researching the field. It was then I realized Public Health made sense to combine my passion for prevention and using my lived experiences to educate others (also confirmed in my birth chart). As I had just begun my first semester a California State University, Dominguez Hills and I was studying for my major, Chicana/o Studies, I had begun to realize that socioeconomic and generational factors can affect certain groups of people regarding accessing supportive resources. It was then I realized that my focus would be attaining an MPH after the completion of my bachelor's degree.

Fortunately, working for a non-profit in Echo Park working with Gang Reduction and Youth Development (GRYD), helped prepare me for grad school. While working there, where I quickly realized how strength-based "brainstorming" could be a powerful tool to determine what support system the youth had in place. We worked with other community-based organizations and local police department to collaborate productively and efficiently. The stress from so much pressure to produce caused me to have my first alopecia areata outbreak. I started to engage in self-care (including massages and removing toxic people, food, and products) to minimize those occurrences since they were stress-induced, and partly due to genetics.

My grandparents never had yearly physicals, as I did, because they lived a rural lifestyle that didn't include regular doctor visits. Their lack of prevention caused both of my grandparents to now have to be seen monthly, by various specialty doctors. Since I am now a mother and have realized the importance of having healthy habits and my need to inform the youth of the importance of increasing prevention of ailments later in life. I am pleased to share that my dream as a student worker that began in 2009 of residing on the west side, on my own, is now a reality! This took some time to accomplish, but I made it happen. We often think the grass is greener on the other side, but the grass is truly green wherever you are grateful.

Becoming a parent has been such a gift by making me hyperaware of the way I affect those around me. My compassion, empathy, and patience increased for others and myself. I learned what love truly means. I used to envision the fairy tale version of love, which was not beneficial to my spiritual evolution and led me to much disappointment. Healing is a process that will cause you to be more in tune with yourself, and less tolerant of those who lack accountability. I am by no means perfect, and I am always learning something new. What matters most is that I am seeking support from individuals who I know are at a higher capability than I am.

Looking at ourselves objectively can cause guilt to arise because you realize that your parents are humans, too. You remove them from the pedestal you once had them on, or you may even stop villainizing them due to their limitations. We feel bad for pointing out the ways our environment and our experiences negatively shaped us, but there is nothing wrong with looking at your past objectively. You may be able to make sense of the stories you have been telling yourself about your upbringing. I now consider how my family did not have the time to learn tools and skills to reflect as I now do.

One may feel obligated to hold parents and family on a pedestal due to their sacrifices, but they're human just like us, and full of free will and self-expression. That means that what they do, may not be beneficial to us because it is impossible to instinctually know what our loved one's desire and need. We may assume they know because we "came from" them. We may come through our parents, but we are not here to live for them. Some people may not agree, but I strongly suggest you explore your "reason" for being on this planet. Knowing your reason why you do things, will remove the "how" that may block your ability to move forward. You may come to the realization that you are in alignment with your purpose which allows you to live in a constant state of happiness, or the exact opposite. If it's the second part of the previous sentence, it may be time to make some changes to incorporate happiness into your day.

My son is now a teen, and I constantly try to ensure that I clear up any stories he may be harboring. This is the power that we all possess, when we choose ourselves first. It sounds selfish at first especially if you're a Latina since we were taught about *Marianismo* (typically women self-sacrificing for others, esp. family) at a young age and it remains embedded in much of our culture. Some men fall into this too, by being "nice guys," until they don't (or do) get what they want. This is something every human should know; we all possess feminine and masculine traits. It is within yourself that you must find that delicate balance. You are complete all by yourself! If you wait "for someone to complete" you, you'll be waiting for eternity. Furthermore, we all have high or low vibrating traits. This is why I strongly encourage you to look up your birth chart to see where your unique low energies are holding you back and what strengths are innate to you.

If I could gift something to all of you is the gift of radical honesty within yourself, and then it would pour over into all your other relationships. There is so much power in speaking your truth with others in a respectable and honest way. Not only do you honor yourself, but you also inspire others to do the same. This shift will naturally lead to less resentment, frustration, and misunderstanding in relationships because there is an understanding that being your true self is safe.

I know in my upbringing there was little room for expressing our feelings but it's time to shift that narrative if it resonates with you too. Then we wonder why people suppress and numb themselves as soon as they can. Happy hours and weekend escapes glorify escaping our current reality. What helped me shift these behaviors was asking myself if my choices were leading me closer to my long-term goals, or not. That has helped immensely to move differently than how I had been spending my time and energy. After seeing how much I wasted, I realized there was very little return on investment which no longer added up. Nothing is more precious than my time and energy because I cannot get that back.

By focusing on diverse populations instead of individuals, there is a much better chance of minimizing health problems. By focusing on lifetime milestones, levels of education, and generational differences, we can unmask what can be interfering with a healthy life. These factors have impacted my own ability to understand and appreciate what my health means. Not everyone's experience is the same, but there are certain phases that one must endure to outgrow. These experiences are what shape our outlook and can affect us in several ways.

Therefore, I fully understand that we all have the power to help one another by sharing our lived wisdom. It's easier to blame others until we realize we hold all the power over ourselves, and our lives. I lived in the victim mentality for a LONG time. At a certain point, we get tired of our own bullsh!t and decide to change, while some never do. Which one will you choose?

I am fondly grateful to my son, family, friends, and community for being who I needed to become this version of myself.

I am creating many new endeavors and cannot wait to share them with you all!

ABOUT ANNETT VELASQUEZ

Annett Velasquez is an Inglewood native and strongly believes that by investing in youth development, fostering community, while tending to our self-care is the key to true social change. She is devoted to improving Latine nutrition and health outcomes in Los Angeles. Her studies span all over LA, beginning at East Los Angeles College, to completing her Master of Public Health at California State University, Long Beach. She practices indigenous spirituality which helps with grounding, and is extremely proud of her Mexican heritage. She enjoys hiking, taking photographs, and spending quality time with her teenage son, family & friends. Her experience as a first generation has equipped her with the necessary tools for a prosperous outlook on life. Her entrepreneurial spirit also allows her creativity to be shared with the world, as you can see in the second & third link below.

LinkedIn: www.linkedin.com/in/annett-velasquez-05682b113
Vegan Beauty Products: www.nettievee.mymonat.com
Instagram: www.instagram.com/LaTapatiaSalsa
www.instagram.com/NettyVMPH

8
EDILKA ANDERSON & CARLA GUZMAN

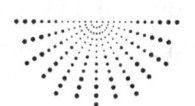

This is a story of faith, family, and the power of friendship. Of two women who were brought together by a force greater than themselves, who chose to take their destiny into their own hands, who embraced their innate passion, strength, loyalty, and dedication to meet adversity with grace. Their story is a reminder that it's never too late to begin again, that we are all a work in progress, and that together, we are so much more powerful than we are alone. This is the story of Edilka and Carla—the paths they've walked individually, what they built together, and the future they're manifesting.

From an early age, Edilka could remember feeling like an outsider, observing the people around her, and never really feeling like she belonged. As a little girl growing up in Panama, Edilka was introverted and insecure, afraid to speak up and share her opinions, but also had the sense that she was meant for something bigger. She loved art and design and would create her own world inside her bedroom, fantasizing about owning a furniture store one day.

Growing up as the eldest with two younger brothers to look after, she was always taught that family came first, but when her parents decided to pack up their lives and move to Canada when she was 11 years old, she felt she had no voice—a wound that would stay with her for many years. Settling into a new life in Canada as part of an immigrant family was difficult, and Edilka struggled with feelings of unworthiness and anxiety throughout her teenage years. She sought out validation and love in her relationships and met the man who would eventually become her husband at 19 years of age. Marcus was a decade older, more established, and came from a remarkable, loving family that Edilka admired, and she believed she had finally met someone who would take care of her and make her feel safe and secure.

Edilka completed her education studying business administration and started to create a future with Marcus by her side. Marcus was charismatic, wildly entrepreneurial, and had big dreams of changing the world. After getting married at 23 years of age, Edilka and Marcus began to grow their family while navigating the ups and downs of marriage. They had three wonderful and beautiful children together, Hayden, Evan, and Sofia, and while on the outside they may have appeared to have it all, Edilka struggled with her own feelings of worth and began to feel like the road she wanted to walk wasn't the same path Marcus was choosing.

The day-to-day pressures and responsibilities of marriage and having children so early on in her life—along with juggling a full-time job in addition to working alongside Marcus, consulting for his digital marketing business—hadn't allowed her the time and space to truly understand who she was before falling into the role of wife and mother. There was a fierceness and fire within her that was calling to be released. One day she woke up and realized she was doing a job that didn't fulfill her, married to somebody who didn't love her the way she knew she deserved, and she wanted more. Edilka felt in her heart it was time to make a change.

Her job in the public sector provided stability and security, but it didn't make her happy—and after years of raising her three children, feeling alone in her marriage, and putting her needs second, she knew that she had to take a leap. She was no longer willing to be a passive observer in her life. She didn't want to just accept being comfortable; she wanted to be inspired, to do something that lit her up from within and made her feel like she was using her skills and passions. Edilka knew there were two things that made her heart sing: fashion and design. After exploring several options, she decided to pursue the world of design and enrolled in a home staging certification program. Edilka hit the "Submit" button for the course and prayed that she was making the right choice by following her intuition.

Meanwhile, Carla was also navigating changes in her own life, something she was no stranger to. Since moving from her birthplace in Chile to Venezuela at 7 years of age, she had spent the formative years of her childhood moving from city to city for her father's work, leaving behind friends and having to adapt to new environments constantly. Despite the challenges that came with being unanchored, Carla loved the people, culture, and spirit of Venezuela and truly felt her soul belonged in the vibrant country. She went to Caracas to study economics at the age of 16 and felt like she was thriving, making meaningful friendships, and working in the fashion industry with big dreams for her future. Just a few months later, her dreams were shattered when her parents made the difficult decision to move their family to Canada, and like Edilka, Carla was forced to pack up and say goodbye to a life she wasn't ready to leave.

Arriving in Canada at 17, Carla struggled to find her place. While she had already been studying at the university level in Venezuela, she was forced back into the high school system in Canada, and she felt out of touch with the language, the culture, and the people. Nevertheless, she persevered and tried to maintain the positive attitude her parents had taught her to cultivate, actively pursuing new opportunities for a better life. She began working as a flight attendant upon completing her education, travelling across Europe and experiencing the world with an insatiable sense of curiosity. On a holiday visit back to Venezuela, Carla met Domingo, fell in love, and serendipitously moved back to South America to start a new chapter of her life for the next 21 years.

Life in Venezuela was amazing. Carla felt she was finally at home, in a country she loved and felt she belonged to, building a family and a livelihood the way she had always imagined. She and her husband Domingo had two beautiful daughters together, Stephanie and Valerie, and she launched a rich and diverse career running exhibitions and trade shows across the country featuring fashion, music, and art, offering a platform for people to showcase their talent. She felt she was following her passion, learning, and growing constantly in her work, with roles spanning across PR, media, marketing, events, and more. She even had the opportunity to host her own TV show talking about health, mindfulness, beauty, fashion, and travel. Unfortunately, as political tensions increased in the country, Carla and her husband realized they had to protect their family, and they made the hard choice for Carla to uproot her life and move to Canada with their children while Domingo stayed behind to run his family business, promising to join them there when the time was right.

Coming back to Canada after 21 years of living her dreams abroad, Carla was grieving the life she had left behind and unsure of what lay ahead for her. Domingo was an amazing husband and father and giving up their life in Venezuela together felt like a huge sacrifice for her. As much as she hoped her husband would join their family soon, a part of her heart wondered if he was truly willing to leave his life behind as she had. At 44 years of age, with two daughters to care for and a long-distance husband, she felt like a newcomer again. With yet another chance for a fresh start, she felt compelled to follow her passion for beauty, travel, and real estate and find a way to bring more joy into the world. As a way to understand every facet of the real estate industry, she signed up for a Home Staging Certificate, which would also give her the chance to make connections and lay the foundation for herself and her family in a country that didn't quite feel like home. Carla's parents had always instilled in her the importance of being adaptable and optimistic, of seeing changes as opportunities and fresh starts, and she was determined to move forward with resilience and a positive outlook.

Unaware of the parallels in their lives, the two women met on the first day of the staging course and immediately felt they had found a kindred spirit in one another. Beyond instinctively being drawn to each other's energy, they discovered they had so much in common; both being Latina, being mothers, and having an appreciation for art, culture, and design. They had both been married at 23 years of age. They were adventurous and ambitious. They were deeply rooted in their faith and spirituality, and this was the beginning of a new chapter in their lives.

After completing the course in early 2017, Edilka and Carla independently started their own ventures, and their friendship continued to blossom. Edilka ended up establishing Interiors and Impressions and left her job to pursue styling and staging full-time. Carla launched CG Renovations and Designs, focusing on renovation and interior design projects. They would call one another for advice or support on a project, lifting each other up and laughing their way through whatever challenges came their way. They were reclaiming the voices they felt they had lost as young women and creating life on their own terms as Latinas rising, and it was beautiful.

One day in late 2017, Edilka found herself walking past a KARE Design store in her neighborhood and immediately felt drawn to their unique home furnishings and accessories, stirred by her childhood dream of having a furniture store. She walked in and introduced herself to the owner and was offered a role as a consultant, which then led to the opportunity for her to take over ownership of the store in early 2018. By then, she had separated amicably from her husband Marcus after many failed attempts to bridge the growing divide between the two of them and was trying to find the balance between being a business owner and a mother of three.

When Edilka thought of making her dream come true and becoming a KARE franchise owner, she knew that it was more than she could take on alone—and could think of no better person to join forces with than her friend Carla, who had the perfect combination of skills and experience to complement her in this new business endeavour. She picked up the phone and together the two women decided to take the leap to become business partners in Interiors and Impressions, focusing their energy on KARE and writing a new chapter together in a true act of faith.

Immediately, Edilka and Carla threw themselves into the store, rolling up their sleeves and pouring all their efforts into making it a success. They planned a grand opening party in September 2018 with a public debut at Canada's largest national home show lined up the following day and felt their hearts swell as they looked around a room surrounded by family and friends who were there to support and cheer them on. How far they had both come from just a year and a half earlier when they were feeling lost, confused, and unclear of their path. How much they had achieved. They had worked hard to take their lives into their own hands and make their dreams come true. They felt blessed to have been drawn to one another, trusting in the flow of life. Unfortunately, tragedy struck unexpectedly the next day, when Marcus—a seemingly fit, young, healthy man—suffered a sudden heart attack while loading a truck for the home show and collapsed into Carla's arms, dying almost instantly.

In that moment, time stopped. As Carla held Marcus in her arms, she could hear voices and sirens around her, but all she could feel so vividly was the fragility of life. How could something like this happen? Why now? What would come next?

Death. Birth. The circle of life continued turning. As Edilka was rebuilding her career and emerging into the next evolution of herself, she lost her husband. The father of her children. Her biggest cheerleader. A man she had known and loved for nearly two decades. While they had been separated for the past few years, he was still a constant presence in her life, and his passing left a massive void. Edilka was brought to her knees. And immediately, Carla was there to lift her up. Carla, who had been the last person Marcus saw and spoke to before he died. Carla, who said to Edilka: "Hold my hand.

Everything is going to be fine. I've got this. Go deal with your kids, sit with your grief, and I'll take care of the store and this business until you are ready to stand again."

And despite the anguish and heartbreak, it was at that moment that Edilka felt truly supported. Safe. Seen. Cared for. She knew then that in Carla she had found a true partner, someone with whom she was able to let go and trust that she would be held up. And a few years later, when Carla's husband still had not made the move to Canada and the strain of broken promises and distance on their 25-year marriage became too much to bear—Edilka was there, supporting Carla through her divorce. Saying "I've been there. I understand. I'm here for you." Being a shoulder to cry on and a pillar of strength. Carla loved her husband, but it was time to move on and step fully into her new life in Canada.

Through all of life's challenges, they continued building their business together. They worked long hours, managed a team, and maintained a beautiful showroom. They went on buying trips to Europe. Against all odds, their business survived COVID while so many other stores around them shut their doors. When the neighbourhood began changing, they relocated the store to a new city and started fresh yet again. Yet no amount of hard work and willpower could change the reality of the situation: the retail landscape had changed. The market wasn't responding. Sales weren't where they needed to be, and ultimately, they came to a point where they had to make a decision: do they keep trying or walk away?

Mentally, physically, financially, and emotionally, Edilka and Carla were drained. They had experienced death and divorce, poured everything they had into KARE, and it just wasn't working. They made the decision together that it was time to move on. There is a time for everything in life: a time to hold on and a time to let go, and they had gained the wisdom of living their way into the answer that felt the most authentic and true for them, no matter how difficult. A chapter that once began as a beautiful dream come true ended with the closing of their doors in January of 2024.

While the business didn't survive the way they had originally envisioned, their partnership and friendship still thrive, and they continue to build and grow Interiors and Impressions. If it wasn't for KARE, Edilka and Carla wouldn't have been brought together. They gained a best friend, a business partner, a soulmate, a sister, and so many priceless memories and experiences. All of the relationships they built and honored in their journey lay the foundation for their future success. And along the way, Carla found love again in her fiancé James, reminded once again that the Universe works in mysterious ways, and that people are brought into our lives exactly when we need them.

Two women set off on a voyage of truth and self-discovery, and trusted life enough to bring them together. Their faith was stronger than their fear. Through all of life's ups and downs, Edilka and Carla have been a constant force in one another's lives, embodying the leaning on and leaning in between two partners. From losing loved ones to dreaming up new business ideas, they have experienced a rebirth of themselves and their identities as women, mothers, sisters, and daughters. They transmuted their trauma and turned it into an opportunity for expansion, choosing to undertake a true internal revolution in the process. Today, they spend their days laughing and living life to the fullest, because they understand and appreciate just how valuable it is to be healthy, to be alive, and to have opportunities to share their passions with the world.

Through death, divorce, and dissolving their business, Edilka and Carla have witnessed one another accept all the cards they were dealt, both good and bad, with grace and dignity. They were reminded that women contain multitudes, including the power to be soft and strong at the same time. Now, they dream of making an even bigger impact by launching a virtual staging and design education platform. Edilka and Carla are excited to share their knowledge, wisdom, and lessons learned to teach, inspire, and lead others around the world into their own journey of starting a business and finding their place in the design and real estate industries as they did, cultivating their purpose and passion along the way.

Were there bumps in the road? *Claro que si.* In the words of Confucius: "Our greatest glory is not in never falling, but in rising every time we fall." There is never the perfect time to do anything. With a little bit of trust and faith, you find yourself being led to the answers...sometimes in surprising and unexpected ways. Feel the fear and do it anyway. There is still so much to be written, and life is worth living to the fullest.

ABOUT EDILKA ANDERSON & CARLA GUZMAN

Edilka Anderson and Carla Guzman are the co-founders of Interiors and Impressions, a leading design firm dedicated to creating captivating, luxurious spaces that blend innovation with personality. Hailing from Panama and Venezuela respectively, the two women have combined their diverse backgrounds and decades of experience across business, art, fashion, and media to create a boutique design consultancy committed to shaping beautiful, uplifting spaces that foster connection. Their work includes luxury home staging and curated designs for commercial and residential interior spaces. Fuelled by faith, family, and friendship, Edilka and Carla continue to evolve their business and themselves, integrating and sharing the lessons they've learned through their individual and shared journeys, diving deeper into their passion for spiritual growth, living their values, and finding their higher calling. They are proud Latinas, mothers, daughters, sisters, and friends.

Website: *www.interiorsandimpressions.com*
Email: *info@interiorsandimpressions.com*
Facebook: *www.facebook.com/interiorsandimpressions*
Instagram: *www.instagram.com/interiorsandimpressions*

9

JASMINE MURUDUMBAY

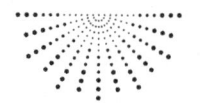

LATINA IN RECOVERY

Do you remember your first kiss? I do.

My first kiss was in an elevator. I was alone at first, then he came on. I was nervous. I had these feelings rumbling inside. These feelings often came up and I didn't know what to do with them. I spent most of my childhood shoving them down. There was a strange feeling in the elevator. This feeling was new. I never felt like this before. Then it happened: He leaned over and kissed me. He kissed me long enough to feel that this was not what I wanted. If he was a boy that I liked, I would have run home to tell my sister. I would have remembered it as one of the greatest moments. I would have remembered my first kiss with that boy. But he wasn't a boy and he was a grown man. He was a stranger that I never saw on the elevator again. For years it felt like it was a dream or something I made up.

I didn't run home to tell anyone what just happened. I didn't run home to tell someone I just had my first kiss. I got out of the elevator and ran into our apartment. We lived on Sumach St. Our area is known as Regent Park. Our building was 605 Whiteside Rd. This address is stapled in my memory and I remember it like a song that you can't stop singing. Our building had sadness, violence, perverts, yelling, cops, and fear. I would hear fighting, shouting and cops around. There was this feeling that I shouldn't feel safe here. I wasn't safe here. I wasn't safe anywhere. The only safe place I found was within me. I learned to keep quiet. Keeping quiet was my safe place. Not being seen and heard. Being quiet kept me safe. I didn't want anyone to know what happened to me. I thought maybe it was my fault, that somehow, I had done something or said something to make him kiss me. If I stayed quiet about what happened, I couldn't be blamed, questioned, or attacked for it.

Hiding and staying quiet became my safe haven.

It was easy to stay quiet where I grew up. This was expected of me. Growing up in our Ecuadorian home, we were taught that good little girls should stay quiet and respectful. You don't disrespect your parents and elders. Only the girls with the big mouths are the troublemakers. Tienes que estar callada. No dices nada a nadian. I thought being a good little girl was something you had to do and become. If you were good, then good things will happen to you. You would know you were good by getting people's approval. They would validate that I was a good girl. When they did, I felt better about myself. I could like and accept myself. I constantly chased people's praise and love. When I didn't get it, I made it mean that there was something wrong with me. I was constantly trying to fix myself.

Growing up I felt fea. I felt like no one thought I was pretty. No one really paid attention to me. It was like I didn't exist. I remember my sister always getting the praise. She was thin. I wasn't. I was jealous of her beauty and thinness. We would wear similar clothes, most of the clothes we had were her size. I had a belly with buttons coming out.

Going to school, I felt like people could see it and I spent the whole day trying to cover my belly. Anxiety and worry took over my body while I was trying to be like my classmates. I hated being overweight. I hated being me. If I was a different person then I wouldn't have to feel like this every day. I wished I was my sister. I wished I was a thin little girl. I wished I was anyone but me. I didn't wish to be another fat little girl. They have problems like me too. I want to be like the pretty white girls that don't have the same life I do. I used to feel bad about it. I thought, "How could I be so envious?". I remember hearing, no tienes que ser envidiosa. I felt ashamed to feel emotions that I was told were wrong to feel. I felt ashamed to feel anything at all because most of the time I felt "bad" emotions. It was hard to feel something so natural like envy and not feel bad about it. When you experience trauma and addiction growing up, it is hard as a child to feel happy emotions. I used to see other girls my age and I felt so jealous of them. I was always comparing their outsides to my insides. I thought If I had their lives, I wouldn't feel so bad all the time. I chased the belief that once I had everything I wanted, then I would feel good inside. I was missing out on a father, good clothing, school lunches that were more than ketchup sandwiches and tang, gifts at Christmas or birthdays, or living in a house. I wanted my mom to be home to spend time with us instead of working two jobs to make sure we had enough. A mom that wasn't stressed out and tired. I was always hoping and waiting for life to feel better. I waited for someone to come to fix my life so I could feel better.

It wasn't until I had my first drink that things started to change for me inside. When I had the taste of my first drink, something happened. Something that I never felt like before. I didn't feel bad about myself. I didn't remember how I grew up. The unwanted kisses.

The absent father. The anger. The violence. The drinking. The shame.

Alcohol took away the pain I had been feeling since I was a child. I could breathe again. I became pretty. I was thin. My skin colour didn't matter, I didn't feel so afraid of life. I didn't think about who I was and how I didn't measure up. Alcohol helped to tuck it in the safe little place. At least this is what it felt like. What I was really doing was going into blackouts from the moment I started drinking. The first drink gave me the rush, gave me ease from anxiety and I wanted to keep feeling this way so I kept drinking until eventually I went into blackouts. Drinking became my safe haven.

When I drank, I could express how I was really feeling. My feelings came up easily. Almost too easy that it came up in extremes. I would either be sad and cry for hours or be angry and want to fight people.When I wasn't drinking, I knew that at the end of the week, I would drink to release how I was feeling. I was a binge drinker so I thought I didn't have a problem because only people that drank every day had a problem. I only drank on Fridays and Saturdays. On the weekends.

I told myself I work and I am responsible. I deserve to drink.I was responsible for work but not for my life and family. When I was responsible it was the bare minimum or because I was forced into it.

I drank without feeling any responsibility. I blamed others for my drinking.

I blamed others for my life.

I was a people pleaser. I was constantly doing what other people asked or what they wanted. I was raised to never question what your parents or a man wants you to do. This spilled out to other people. If they asked you, you can't say no. You accommodate them. You do what you're told.

I showed one side to the world.

I showed one side to my family.

Inside I was another person. I walked around feeling like a bad person. It was as if there was a dark cloud following me around. I even had a name for it. Shadoe. Shadoe was my familiar comfortable place.Alcohol helped me to not be the quiet girl.

Drinking helped the lonely quiet girl craving attention get attention from men.I grew up believing that men could do whatever and you would have to take it. You had to be submissive. Learning that men could do whatever is a painful wound that took a long time to heal. It took hours of talking to therapists, loved ones, trusted friends, and a sponsor. Asking questions. Crying alone and with others. Becoming open to healing so that I could feel better about myself and how I grew up. I used the word "Whatever" because I often heard "He does whatever he wants." Not knowing what whatever means, my definition was, "A man could touch you, have sex with you, hit you, stalk you, ignore you, leave you, verbally attack you, cheat on you." Whatever could mean many different things to us as a Latina women. My whatever was an endless list. Each time a man did whatever, I would add it to my list of what I was supposed to accept and not say anything or do anything about it and just make sure he didn't get out of control. I believed I was the reason why he was like that. If I couldn't control him then it was because I wasn't good enough to change. If he did something to me it was because I must have done something wrong. My job was to pick up the pieces after he did whatever. Be the strong woman who could overcome whatever and tell people your suffering and how you overcame it despite what happened.

One story I remember as a little girl was watching my dad drunk and crying. I don't remember why he was crying but I remember being told to go over to him and give him a hug so he could stop crying. I did what I was told. He didn't stop. He started crying more. He kept drinking. I remember thinking, you couldn't stop him from crying. Your own dad. You didn't fix him. You are the problem. If you were good enough, he would have stopped.

It left a hole that could only be filled by men when they said I was good enough.

A hole that had me chase love, ignore the red flags, and lose a part of myself.

At 16, I became a teen mom. I thought I had the love you see in movies. Boy meets the girl; they fall in love and live happily ever after. That didn't happen. When I found out I was pregnant, my mom said she would take care of me and my baby but that I would have to leave my boyfriend. Scared and not knowing what my future was going to be like. I said yes to my mom and cut it off with the love of my life. I told him to leave, but I couldn't get rid of him so easily.

Eventually he left. He left to commit crimes that eventually gave him 5 years in the Pen.

Devastated, I followed him into the Pen, with my daughter in my arms and hungover most of the time. I would go see him. He controlled me while he was in jail. I didn't see anyone but him. We had our phone calls, our letters, and our love while he was serving time. I didn't want to break my little family apart. I didn't want my daughter to be fatherless the way I grew up. I forced things to happen so my daughter wouldn't experience the same pain I did. That didn't work. I stayed in the toxic relationship. Being yelled at, threatened for my life, and feeling like a failure, I drank to soothe the pain. I self medicated at every chance I could.

I worked, studied, drank, and spent less time with my daughter.

I felt deep inside that she was better off with my mom and her grandparents taking care of her than I was. The feelings of being a bad person haunted me and now I was going to do this to my little girl. I would rather her feel the pain of my absence than treat her poorly. When we did spend time together, I was tired from work or hungover from partying too much. I would let her play while I drank more. Treating her to meals. We had our local Chinese restaurant where the locals would go eat food, but mostly drink. It was like a bar. I walked in tipsy and left drunk.

Safety was not my priority. What alcohol addiction does is take away the ability to make sound judgment. I needed to feed my craving to drink. As a mom, I have made choices that have caused pain.

This is where my addiction took me. This is where my drinking took my family.

I lived many years in the cycle of feeling bad about myself, drinking, trying to change it, feeling like nothing was changing, and drinking again. Drinking because I failed my partner, my kids, and myself. I wished I was someone else because if I was someone else, I would be able to stop. I lived in constant fear, anger, sadness and people-pleasing. It wasn't until a few things happened that made me realize that drinking was hurting me. I didn't see it until I stopped drinking. Once I put the alcohol down. The healing process began not only for me but my kids and my family.

When shame became greater than my hangovers and the alcohol stopped working, I started to see how my drinking was making me feel. I couldn't look at myself in the mirror anymore. If I did, it was to scream negative words to myself. I started to feel the shame vibrate in my body. I felt like I was a walking open book and everyone could see that I had been drinking. Calling in sick on a Monday became my norm. I started to behave the way I saw my dad behaving to my family. I would disappear for hours only to come back drunk and drink more or pass out. I put all the responsibilities on my partner. The dark cloud that disappeared when I drank was constantly following me around. My daughter, 18 at the time, at a party, told me I was drunk. She didn't use those words but the message was there. This time I heard her. At the time of the party, I was mad at her for talking back to me this way. Her mom!

I swore that I wouldn't do to my kids what I grew up with. I was doing it. It was now in my face that I had turned into someone I never wanted to be like. I had caused it. I finally started to feel the tiredness of what my kids and my partner saw. At that moment, I saw the choices I had been making. I couldn't run away. I couldn't drink. I was done. I didn't know what to do. I didn't know what to say. I called my sister, the person who I trusted the most, and told her I needed help.

My journey began at the moment that I realized I was done and needed help. I had moments when I woke up thinking "Maybe you do have a problem." At that point, I wasn't convinced. It wasn't until I was sure that I had a problem with drinking that I started to make changes. I had tried many times to stop drinking but this time, it felt different. My addiction counsellor planted the seed of ways to get sober. When she first mentioned joining a recovery group. I was like I only know it from When a Man Loves a Woman or TV shows. I didn't know anything about recovery, treatment centres, or any way to stop drinking. I thought people just stopped and they would be fine. I joined a recovery group. I saw people that didn't look like me or people that drank in my life. They didn't look like they had a drinking problem. I was shocked to see not only Latinos drank. Addiction hits all races, classes, ages, and homes.

I started to learn about my drinking in my recovery group.

I started to learn about myself through my sponsor. A woman that had been where I have been with her drinking.

I made friends.They understood me because they felt the way I did.

It was the first time I felt seen and heard.

It was the first time I felt seen and heard about my pain.

It was the first time I felt seen and heard about my drinking.I started to get to know myself without the drinking.

I started to get to know myself.

Growing up in a home where there was fighting, drinking, and violence, I learned how to deal with life without drinking, screaming, hitting, or manipulating. Step by step, like a baby walking for the first time, I learned. Fell and got back up.

I learned that it wasn't my fault that my first kiss was taken from me, but that I could heal. I learned to take responsibility for my own actions, and to give people their own responsibility for their actions. I learned how to not mix the two up.

I learned that healing is part of my journey of recovery from addiction, trauma, and love.

Healing is a part of our family's journey and for future generations.

For me, healing has been about living in the moments that come up and facing them.Facing them sober today.Today I am a Latina in Recovery.

ABOUT JASMINE MURUDUMBAY

Jasmine Murudumbay is a Latina in Recovery coach. She coaches Latinas in their journey to stop drinking by helping them connect to their story and change the drinking narrative in their lives. As a woman in recovery from alcohol addiction, she has changed the drinking narrative in her family and future generations. Her narrative that includes Recovery is possible.

Website: *www.lifeinrecovery.net*
Email: *jaz@lifeinrecovery.net*
Instagram: *www.instagram.com/latinainrecoverycoach*

10
JESSICA CORONADO

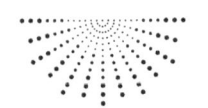

Not much is known about my father's side of the family. Both of my paternal grandparents passed away when my father was rather young. My maternal grandmother came from sixteen kids, my maternal grandfather from seventeen, my father from thirteen, and my mother from five. My great grandma was a cook for the farm workers in a labor camp's kitchen and my grandma would help her. And with all of her siblings that kept being born, my grandma eventually had to drop out of school to help with caring and providing for the younger kids as well. In the older generations, it's what was done. It's how families survived. My grandpa got as far as 1st grade. He was here working and sending money back home to Mexico at the age of 12.

My mom and dad were junior high school sweethearts. They had big dreams after high school to get married with my dad going into the service and my mom becoming a nurse. However, things changed when my father fell into addiction. It was common for the neighborhood we were in, it was part of the culture. It was something many of the neighbors, family, and friends eventually succumbed to in that era. The neighborhood was filled with addictions of all sorts. My dad started with weed and ended with heroine. It played out over many years, and he did what addicts did to get by, which resulted in a lot of jail time. I remember sitting in the house in the dark with my mom and my siblings because they shut the lights off due to non-payment.

My dad's best friend, Mike, came by with some McDonald's for us once. My mom would walk us to and from school every day. One day, when she came to pick us up she said she had a surprise for us. We lived a few blocks from the school so we excitedly tried to get home as fast as we could. When he got there... the surprise was dad. He was home from jail. Don't get me wrong, it was a great surprise. That's just where we were with how often he was at "The Holiday Inn' as he would call it. I do have many memories of my dad when I was little, but I will admit that most of the fun ones are after my parents' split when I was 5. After being married for 9 years and having 4 kids together, my mom took us away from dad and the neighborhood, and cried the whole time she packed our bags. My dad would later say it was the best thing she's ever done for him. In my little girl brain though, for many years, I saw it as my dad leaving us. I walked around with what I thought were daddy issues of abandonment.

My mom later remarried and had my youngest brother. That made us a family of 7. We had moved to a typical working-class neighborhood, consisting mostly of minorities. Lots of single parents, but even the married couples had to both work. A lot of us kids were left to take care of ourselves and each other while all the parents worked. We were the latchkey kid generation. It was awesome for the most part, so much freedom for everyone in general. Not so much for me, though.

In our household, my parents were very traditional of girl vs boy roles. Us kids were roughly 2 years apart. I was 14 years old with an older brother and 3 younger siblings beneath me. I had started to resent that role more and more over the years, but I think so much happened that particular year that led to a house full of kids during the summer and things went totally haywire. Both parents were working a lot, my mom had her own hair salon at the time. Plus, they were taking a marital break with my stepdad moving out of the house for a bit while they worked on things. My parents basically supplied all the necessities to run the house and I was left in charge of managing it all. I hated it. I needed help and to be looked after too, I was still a kid.My parents were not malicious with intent or causing me pain or harm when they had me watching my siblings. They were just carrying on what they had been programmed to do by generations before them. They were repeating what their parents did. But the way I seen it was, I did not want kids. And here I was left to care for kids that were not mine even though I kept saying it wasn't fair. Why me?? Why does all the responsibility always fall back on only me? And I always got, "Because you're the oldest girl." Nothing pissed me off more than hearing those words.

Unfortunately, I never figured out how to shut it off, so it overflowed over my entire life, and I carried that responsibility well into my forties. I took on stuff that wasn't mine. It expanded to my whole family and even close friends. I became a people pleaser. Granted, it was all a choice. But at the time, I didn't know that. As I've sought healing on all levels, these buried resentments are being uncovered and forgiven as I realize my parents were learning as well and doing the best with what they had at the time. I could also spend my days playing the blame game with my exes... he was mean, he took advantage, he did me dirty. But I also have to take ownership of seeing the red flags and choosing to ignore them. I was no longer a victim—I was a participant.

One of the greatest things about taking ownership is you get your power back. You can stay in the victimhood mentality, or you can reframe it. You get to say no and stop the cycle. Right then and there you can decide to react differently. You don't have to stay in the mindset of, "I'm just wired this way. I've been this way my whole life." No, not true. Once we start healing and working through issues, we can learn new healthier ways to react and be. It takes some getting used to, but it's truly exciting to discover different parts of yourself that exist beneath the onion you start peeling back.

Growing up with my "daddy issue" of abandonment, every romantic relationship was the same. They all ended the same. All were with the same person. Emotionally unavailable... them and me. I knew it. I expected it. And, for the most part, I was okay with it. Until I wasn't. One relationship came along that was different. And I wanted to know why. I had put up such a fight at the end, determined to make it work because something in my gut told me this was for love. I could feel such a strong pull. LOVE, LOVE, LOVE. While it felt like that, as parts of me began to heal, I began to realize that it could not be love because the relationship was insanely toxic.

At this time in my life, I was learning about God and universe and divine timing and how everything lines up for my highest good. As it turns out... yes... that particular relationship was sent to teach me about love. But not love of a man... but love of SELF. Two weeks after the breakup, I was diagnosed with stage 2 breast cancer. Six months before meeting this man (3 years prior), I had lost my dad. After the breakup, it all felt compacted—the loss of my dad, the loss of love, the loss of my health, all of it came crashing down and I was falling backwards into a black abyss with nothing to grab on to. It was frightening beyond anything I had ever experienced.

My dad came to know God in his last 25 years of life. When he talked about God, he was so grateful to be rescued from his old life that he spoke of it freely to whoever, whenever. He always wanted to be helpful in that way. Because everything had been lost. His jobs, our house, his family, his children, his marriage, everything was gone. He had nothing left. When he began to get pieces of his life back little by little, there was immense gratitude there. He was always thankful to The Father. That's how he addressed God. After he got sick and was transitioning, we were his caretakers.

Seeing him live out his last days was a sight to be seen. Knowing the life he lived and seeing him at total peace while he waited to slip away, it made me want that for myself. Because his life from what I remembered it being, to what it now became, was night and day. My dad had a beautiful life and because of that, I already knew God to be real. We had a great relationship; we were very close. I loved watching him be "Dad" again, like he was before all the bad stuff happened. He lived his life by example of God's mercy and grace and what that can do to a person. Towards the end, listening to dad talk about how he was ready to go, it made me envision a place for him that I'd want to go to too one day. How about that? The man that I had felt had abandoned me a large part of my life turned out to be the man to lead me to my Heavenly Father. We talked about God often. He was so patient, he answered all my questions as best as he could.

Originally diagnosed with stage 2 breast cancer in 2015, in remission until 2019, then diagnosed with stage 4 with metastasis to lungs. They initially gave me 18 months if I did nothing as far as prognosis was concerned. If I jumped on their regimen of conventional treatment, they gave me 5 years if I "was lucky." I decided to take my chances with holistic and alternative modalities. Covid hit a year in, making things even more complicated. My lymph nodes were inflamed and closing in on my throat, causing me to lose my voice for about 6 months. Towards the end of the summer, my church had an alter call for healing. My pastor and his wife applied holy oil and prayed over me with some other church members. Nothing happened that night. But in the morning? My voice was back! Literally overnight, God had restored my voice. There were no new treatments, no new meds, nothing. All God. JUST GOD. That's like a miracle from the bible days. I was stunned. You can't tell me God is not real. And that's how I've been managing my care... on a prayer. I go wherever I'm guided. I'm looking to heal myself on all levels, not just physically. I'm also working on spiritual, emotional, mental, nutritional, all of it. Holistic. It's all connected.

We had actually been baptized as babies and my mom talked to us about God growing up. But we always did everything as a family. Once we were on our own, we didn't go to church anymore. After losing my dad and seeing his transition, I was propelled to find that for myself. I'd visit different churches here and there, but nothing ever felt right. I did eventually find one and start attending and learning about building an actual relationship with God. It was a game changer and I learned so much. For instance, sometimes no matter how hard I prayed, it seemed like I wouldn't get any answers. It would be frustrating and disappointing.

The very first time I had to be admitted to the hospital by myself due to breathing issues, I was sitting in that hospital bed, wondering what it was. What was it? I had never had to be hospitalized before so naturally it was concerning and a bit scary because I was all by myself thanks to covid. Test after test were run and as they came in with the results, I would slash it off my mental list—okay, it's not that. What else could it be? And I would wait until the next results. I had so much anxiety just waiting there like that. Then it occurred to me. You know what? It could be any one of these things—pneumonia, blood clot, covid, infection, etc... and it could kill me. But it has not been a single one of them. So how about rejoicing in THAT? How about rejoicing in what it is not? I am so concerned about solving the puzzle that I am overlooking every blessing I am being given, so I started thanking God for what it wasn't. I was so preoccupied looking for the big blessing that I was missing all the little miracles along the way.

I always thought I was independent and strong. That had been one thing that everyone had complimented me on growing up... that I was super independent. I was proud and wore it like a badge of honor, thinking this is what I've earned after all those years of fighting to be seen. I'm tough. I can take whatever is thrown at me. I'll figure it out, I'll get the job done. Later through therapy, I discovered it was actually a trauma response to feeling abandoned. I assumed the independence role because I had gotten used to not having anywhere else to go. I had no choice but to depend on myself because when I tried to speak up many years ago, telling them that I didn't want to run the house, I was crying, frustrated, angry, sad, and hurt. Feeling unworthy. Unseen. Unheard. And no matter how loud I got, no one cared. No one was coming to see what I needed. My dad left. Then my mom left. And then there was just me. But somehow, hearing that it didn't mean that I had to be strong... it gave me permission to be soft. And that was different. It was nice. Instead of feeling like I had to carry everyone's issues on my shoulders, I could lay them down and just carry my own. Doing work through childhood trauma, which has been incredibly helpful on the emotional level, I've been able to put so many of the puzzle pieces together. When I come across my inner child and there's a wound, I can choose to Love her. I was invited to, "Be there for her. Be the person you needed to be there for you." For years, with the toxic relationships and all of the people pleasing, it was too much. The cancer coming was the only thing that could silence all the noise. It was the only thing that would finally force me to put myself first. In that sense, I see it as cancer coming to save my life not take it. I have to pay attention.

Even as I write this today... I am sitting in a hospital bed. Still going though yet another incident. My faith is strong. And this situation is temporary. Our bodies are designed to heal. It's so very important that we become our own advocates when it comes to our health. Get that 2nd and 3rd opinion. Research for yourself. Go with your gut, listen to your own intuition. When they checked me in here, they thought it was one thing and started treatment for it. When I spoke with several doctors and asked if it could be what I was suspecting, they said possibly. We ran some tests and sure enough, my hunch was right. So, we started treatment and have had some success little by little daily. No one knows your body better than you. If you feel something in your gut, go with it.

I am not afraid to die. And I'm in any rush to. I do hope that I'm here for many more years to come. It doesn't matter what we're labeled as because someone did die today. Someone lost their life. Whether it be by car accident, gunshot wound, plane crash, heart attack. Someone didn't make it today. And they did not have a terminal illness diagnosis. And I have one of those but I'm here still. I made it through another day. So, does it really matter what we're labeled with? Should we really care to pay attention to that? Should we let that hang over our heads and bring us worry? Or should we live our lives the best we can day by day filled with hope and joy as we see it? Because we are still here. Still thriving, still living. We will all die one day, no one is making it out of here alive. It's the cycle of life. And I don't care how many years of medical school someone has, that doesn't give them the right to tell you how long you have left to live. No one knows that.

I'll admit, some days feel unbearable. On those days, I just think back to when I was at the oncologist's office and he said the words stage 4, I knew what that meant. But then I felt and heard another set of words, "That is not my story. My God is greater." I find it very difficult to explain exactly how those words poured into me or where exactly they poured from. But they were certainly alive and very real. I had absolute peace and stillness. Not a single fear whatsoever. There was a steadiness that grounded me, and I knew that I would not be moved. Whenever times get hard, I always go back to that moment and remember who my father is.

ABOUT JESSICA CORONADO

Jessica Coronado is a two-time cancer survivor. First being diagnosed with Stage 2 breast cancer in 2015, then being diagnosed with Stage 4 metastatic lung cancer in 2019. Now coming up on her 10th year in journeying through regaining her health, she's discovering there's so much healing to be done on all levels. Not just the physical... but the spiritual, mental, and especially emotional. It all goes hand in hand. She's been labeled as terminal but that hasn't stopped her from still finding joy and hope in the darkest of places. Her faith in God has carried her through it all. Jessica loves to travel. She took her first trip in her early 20s and hasn't stopped. It's her dream to see the world and all of God's creations. Jessica also loves to paint. It's very therapeutic and is an excellent way to release her creativity.

Website: www.instagram.com/cor_je

11
LILIANA BERNAL

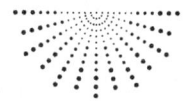

BEING LATINA IS NOT MY LABEL—IT'S MY SUPERPOWER

Sitting poolside, soaking up the sun at the Venetian Hotel in Las Vegas, I found myself reflecting on a conversation I just had with a publisher who asked me to contribute a chapter to this book.

As I gazed at the shimmering water, I grappled with what to share that could truly impact and inspire others. The tranquil setting made me ponder the significance of my experiences and the lessons I've learned, hoping to find the right words to make a meaningful contribution. As someone who values privacy and shuns social media, I was unsure about opening up. Yet, this extravagant girl's trip reminded me of my journey and the superpowers that have shaped my life. This trip was our annual family "girl's" trip with my niece, cousin, and her daughter. The four of us span 4 decades; the twenties, thirties, forties, and fifties. As I observe each one enjoying this trip it takes me back to those stages in my life and how I grew and developed.

In my twenties, I was full of ambition and eager to prove myself. I took risks, made mistakes, and learned valuable lessons about resilience and perseverance. This period was crucial for building my confidence and understanding the importance of hard work.

My thirties were a time of significant professional growth. I honed my skills, took on leadership roles, and began to see the fruits of my labor. This decade taught me the value of strategic thinking and the power of networking.

Entering my forties, I started to focus more on work-life balance and personal fulfillment. I realized the importance of self-care and the need to nurture relationships. This stage helped me develop a more holistic approach to success, understanding that true achievement encompasses both professional and personal well-being.

Now, in my fifties, I find myself in a position to give back and mentor others. I have a wealth of experience to share and a deep appreciation for the journey that has brought me here. This stage is about legacy and making a lasting impact, not just in my career but in the lives of those I support and inspire.

I am the toddler who came to America with her parents, the teen who moved across the country, experienced tragedy at a very young age and the young woman who once spent the night on a Paris park bench flat broke after taking the wrong train was now an entrepreneur staying in this fancy hotel suite. Now running my own business—an award-winning recruiting and workforce consulting company, mentoring and supporting other women entrepreneurs, and traveling the world creating experiences for myself and my loved ones. How did I get to where I am today?

My story begins in Colombia, where I was born. My parents, like many others, sought the American Dream, so we immigrated to the United States when I was three, settling in New York. Growing up bilingual, I effortlessly switched between Spanish and English, a skill that became one of my first recognized superpowers. It allowed me to navigate different cultures and connect with people from diverse backgrounds.

By the time I started school, my mother's immediate family joined us in New York. I was growing up within a very safe bubble and circle of Latinos in a city that was very diverse. I never felt different because we all shared the same culture and traditions. Growing up in a Latino culture is often associated with valuing community and collective well-being over expressing individualism. This fosters a strong sense of belonging and mutual support. At the same time, it is also very difficult to break away from when you grow into becoming an individual and create an identity of your own.

As the only girl and the middle child between two brothers, I learned the art of negotiation and compromise early on. This ability to be personable and adaptable would serve me well throughout my life. However, I also rebelled against the traditional gender roles prevalent in my family—common in the Latino culture. I questioned why I had more chores than my brothers and sought valid explanations. I often wondered why certain behaviors, interests, and responsibilities were assigned to me just because of my gender.

This persistent questioning and endless ingenuity laid the foundation for my leadership skills. My mother and I frequently clashed on this topic, and I often found myself in trouble for not conforming to the status quo. Standing up for my beliefs, even when it led to conflict, built my confidence. I learned to trust my instincts and be assertive in expressing my views.

ADAPTING TO CHANGE: MOVING ACROSS THE COUNTRY

The first major turning point in my life came when I was sixteen. My father, who worked for United Artists, was transferred to Los Angeles. Leaving New York, a place where I felt at home, was daunting. Yet, this move taught me the power of assimilation. Attending a public co-ed high school in California was a stark contrast to my private, all-girls Catholic High School in New York. I became a chameleon, making friends across varying groups and learning to listen deeply to others' stories.

This period honed my superpowers of adaptability and versatility. I embraced the opportunity to reinvent myself, becoming the "new girl from New York" who was curious about everyone and everything. This ability to connect with others would later become a cornerstone of my professional success.

While I was thriving in this new environment, it brought out the realization my family was different. In LA, I found myself without any Latino friends and quickly noticed the differences in our family dynamics. My parents were very strict, and they didn't really trust strangers, so I was not allowed to stay over my friends' houses. On top of that, my parents were struggling with a new and different environment. My mother especially missed her family and circle of close friends.

In LA, the only Latinos I met were Mexican, and I observed that they were treated differently. This is where I first experienced racism, which was a stark contrast to the inclusive environment I was used to in New York. This was my first realization of what it really means to be an immigrant and feel like you are living between two worlds. On one hand, I was trying to adapt to a new city and culture, while on the other, my family was holding on to their roots and the sense of community we had back home. This duality made me more aware of the struggles immigrants face in trying to balance their identity and belonging in a new environment. It was a challenging yet eye-opening experience that deepened my understanding of the immigrant experience and the importance of empathy and acceptance.

As I navigated these changes, I saw myself growing and adjusting to my new environment. I became more resilient and open-minded, learning to appreciate the beauty of diversity and the strength that comes from embracing multiple cultures. I also made an effort to connect with people from various backgrounds, which helped me gain new perspectives and build a diverse network of friends. However, this growth also caused challenges with my immediate family. While I was adapting to new cultures and expanding my horizons, they were stuck in their old ways. This difference in perspectives sometimes led to misunderstandings and conflicts, as they struggled to understand my new experiences and the changes I was going through. Despite these challenges, I continued to value my family's traditions while also embracing the new aspects of my life, striving to find a balance between the two worlds.

FACING TRAGEDY: A CATALYST FOR GROWTH

Just as I was finding my footing, tragedy struck. My older brother, the pride of our family, was killed in a car accident shortly after his college graduation. He was the first person in our family to graduate from college and had been accepted to USC Law School. He had worked so hard and was pursuing his dream of becoming a lawyer. My parents were so proud. As a graduation present, his girlfriend and I chipped in to rent him his dream car, a Corvette, for a trip down the Pacific Coast. That was the car he was killed in. I felt like I had contributed to his death—and the guilt haunted me.

This devastating loss forced me to grow up quickly. My parents were lost and devasted—as was the entire family. Unfortunately, our family fell apart from the weight of grief. My parents gave up. I moved out of my parents' home, determined to forge my own path. I could no longer live surrounded by the pressure—and by the guilt of my brother's loss. I couldn't and I didn't want to take his place. I had to find my own path. My resilience and tenacity emerged as superpowers as I navigated the complexities of adulthood.

I dropped out of college and worked three jobs to make ends meet. I felt like I was floating through life. I was struggling. I didn't know what I really wanted to do or even what I wanted to become. I was angry at life for showing me the harshness of it—the reality of it. I wanted to go back to being young and dreaming. I wanted to go back to the days of thinking anything was possible. I also knew that I felt different from my family. I wanted a different life. I didn't really subscribe to the typical Latino ways I was raised on and knew—getting married to become a wife and mother was not at the top of my list. I wanted freedom for myself. I wanted to find something that felt like it was mine. I found solace and purpose in work, at the age of twenty-two starting a career in human resources at an architectural lighting manufacturing company. Between the office and the warehouse, my bilingual skills and ability to listen deeply to others' stories became invaluable.

My interest in Human Resources began during my high school years while working at a movie theatre. Starting in an entry-level position, I quickly advanced to management, where I gained valuable experience in recruiting and managing employees. This hands-on experience with manual payroll and recruitment paved the way for my career in Human Resources.

During this transformative period in my life, I met a man—a "gringo"—who would become an integral part of my journey. He wasn't just a colleague; he became my best friend, my life companion, and my biggest supporter. Unlike anyone I'd met before, he never made me feel odd or wrong for wanting more. He understood my struggle with feeling different than my family because he experienced the same thing in his own life. Seeing myself through his eyes gave me the strength and confidence to embrace my true self. His unwavering support and understanding allowed me to pursue my dreams without fear of judgment. With him by my side, I felt empowered to fly, to explore new horizons, and to redefine what success and happiness meant for me. His belief in me was the catalyst that propelled me forward, helping me to create a life that was authentically mine.

With encouragement from a mentor, a woman who ran and owned her own staffing company and provided recruiting support to our manufacturing company. I embarked on a career in the staffing industry, where I thrived for over 25 years. I cultivated another superpower—recognizing strengths in people. This skill allowed me to assemble and lead a team that achieved remarkable success. Our team was the most diverse in the company, and it was this diversity that significantly contributed to our success.

For nearly a decade, we were consistently recognized with awards for our outstanding performance, developing and nurturing some of the company's most impactful clients. One of my greatest career achievements is witnessing many of those individuals go on to build highly successful careers of their own. To this day, we fondly reminisce about those special times, realizing there was a unique magic in our team that is hard to replicate elsewhere. The camaraderie and shared vision we had were truly extraordinary, and they remain a cherished part of my professional journey.

CREATING MY OWN TABLE: THE ENTREPRENEURIAL JOURNEY

After dedicating 19 years to a company, my role was eliminated. Rather than viewing this as a setback, I saw it as an opportunity. For the last year, I was at this company, I had been increasingly unhappy, and one of my greatest disappointments was working under a female CEO for the first time, only to realize that women aren't always supportive of each other in the workplace. This experience fueled my passion for supporting other women entrepreneurs and becoming their biggest cheerleader. It taught me the importance of fostering a supportive environment where women can uplift one another, and it inspired me to create spaces where collaboration and encouragement are the norms. Another superpower was realized.

My experience in the recruiting industry and strong reputation, along with my other superpower—the ability to connect with people—helped me build strong relationships with clients and colleagues. This foundation proved invaluable when a tremendous opportunity arose: the chance to start a franchise division for a smaller regional staffing company. The vision was to create business ownership opportunities for individuals like me, who despite their success, often found themselves without a seat at the table. In February 2020, I opened their first franchise office in Sacramento. It felt as though angels were watching over me because, had this opportunity been delayed even slightly, the onset of COVID-19 might have derailed the entire plan. Fast forward over four years later and, not only did we survive, we thrived. My versatility and ability to pivot helped the business grow rapidly, even during the challenges of the COVID-19 pandemic.

The initial strategy was for me to establish the franchise location from scratch and then find an owner to take over, allowing me to start other locations and manage the franchise division as an employee of the franchisor. However, I decided to stay on as the Sacramento owner, effectively creating my own path and embracing the role of an entrepreneur. We became profitable within a year and, in 2023, we were recognized by the *Sacramento Business Journal* as the #3 fastest-growing company in Sacramento as well as named by *Inc.* magazine's 5000 as #35 fastest-growing in the Pacific Region.

When people ask me how I achieved this, I don't have a fancy answer. I relied on my superpowers: resilience, the ability to recruit great people, and trusting my gut. My bilingual skills and ability to connect with diverse individuals were crucial in building a strong, versatile team. This chapter of my life has just begun, and I am grateful I finally found my way and became an entrepreneur, even though I started this journey in my fifties. This journey has taught me that sometimes what seems like an ending is really just the beginning of something extraordinary.

Being Latina is a part of my identity. It's the wellspring of my strength and success. It has empowered me to embrace every challenge and opportunity with confidence and determination. I've learned to integrate the best of both worlds—maximizing opportunities that many people never have. This dual perspective has guided me through life's ups and downs, helping me create a fulfilling path that honors my heritage while honoring myself and my dreams.

As I sit by the pool, contemplating my story, I realize I do have a story to tell. My superpowers are not just traits—they are the essence of who I am. They have guided me through adversity, helped me connect with others, and allowed me to create my own path. Being Latina is not just my superpower; it's the foundation of my strength, resilience, and success.

In addition to enjoying running my company and watching it flourish alongside my team, I am passionate about supporting other women entrepreneurs. Shortly after starting my business, I sought out a community and found my tribe in groups like the National Association of Women Business Owners (NAWBO). I joined the Board in 2021 and became Board President by 2022. This role challenged me in many ways but also helped me develop my voice—a voice I now use to speak for those who are afraid or unsure how to.

I've met many smart, successful, and tenacious women who have not only supported me but also become my friends. That's why I was shocked to learn that out of fourteen million women-owned businesses in the United States, less than 3% generate over $1 million in revenue. This statistic has inspired me to speak out about what a travesty this is. It has motivated me to expand our table to ensure all women entrepreneurs get an equitable piece of the pie—a table where all women support each other and help each other rise and flourish. In sharing my story, I hope to inspire others to embrace their unique superpowers and recognize that labels do not define us. Someone once said, "You were born an original; do not die a copy."

Today, as an entrepreneur recognized for rapid growth, I reflect on the experiences that have shaped my life. Each stage of my life has contributed to my growth in unique ways, shaping me into the person I am today. By sharing my story, I hope to help others find their own path to success, understanding that our experiences, challenges, and triumphs are what truly shape us.

From the moment I was born, I was given a label: Latina. It was a label that carried with it a rich tapestry of culture, history, and expectations. As I grew, I realized that this label was often used to define me, to place me in a box. But I was determined to show the world that being Latina was not just a label—it was my superpower.

ABOUT LILIANA BERNAL

Liliana Bernal is Founder and CEO of Balanced Diversity, a recruiting and workforce solutions provider helping clients build a workforce that is reflective of our communities. Through her work, Bernal is dedicated to helping people thrive and reach their full potential.

She's also passionate about women in business and spent two years as Board President of the Sacramento Chapter of the National Association of Women Business Owners (NAWBO). Today, she remains in leadership because women business owners matter.Prior to becoming a successful business owner herself and founding Balanced Diversity, Bernal was a senior executive at a global billion-dollar staffing company where she put together a successful track record of year-over-year growth and grew the market to becoming the most profitable in the company.

Bernal's most notable achievement is making an impact through becoming a successful entrepreneur. When she's not impacting lives on the job, she's creating memories through travel and shared experiences with family and friends.

Website: www.balanceddiversity.com
LinkedIn: www.linkedin.com/in/lilianabernal712

12
DR. MARISSA VASQUEZ

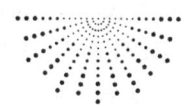

I have never thought of myself as a storyteller, let alone an "author." I typically have a hard time retelling a story, captivating an audience larger than two people, or replaying a funny moment for someone who was not there to witness it firsthand. In contrast, I identify as a "listener" through and through. This is one of the reasons why clinical psychology was a natural career path for me.

Truthfully, when I was approached to write this book chapter, I instantly felt anxious, and my imposter syndrome was activated. I could feel my inner critic awakening and getting loud. Self-doubt was creeping in about taking on this larger public project where I was willingly opening myself up to criticism from others. Harsh, right? But also, I know I am not alone in my experiences with imposter syndrome and learning how to prevent our inner critic from interfering with goals and aspirations. It was challenging for me to see and acknowledge myself as an inspiring Latina of our generation. I can name plenty of other Latinas whose stories I would be interested in reading, who I admire, and who inspire me regularly. But me, my story? No way, Jose.

In Latinx culture, we learn early about "humilidad." Remaining humble and approaching life with humility are seen as positive attributes in our Latinx homes. While there are benefits to our humilidad, I have learned it can also have disadvantages. By that I mean, we are sometimes afraid to speak "too much" about our accomplishments or verbalize ambitious goals at the risk of being seen as "braggy" or "cocky." At the same time, we are often battling internalized racism because it is difficult for us to see ourselves take up space in predominantly White institutions, and imposter syndrome is rooted in feelings of unworthiness and inadequacy.

However, the truth is, as a collective, women of color do not praise themselves enough and need more recognition for all our determination, resiliency, and tenacity. We deserve a seat at the table...you know, the table typically occupied by men and sometimes white women...that table; while it would be ideal for someone with a more privileged identity to recognize that women of color are often missing from said table and ensure we have our metaphorical seat assigned, that is typically not the case. The fact of the matter is we must make that space at the table for ourselves and pull up our own chairs unapologetically. I say, we even place ourselves at the head of the table more often. Okay okay, I'm getting too excited trying to pump you up to be your own girl boss, but you get it, right?

With some thoughtful time and reflection, I recognize I have achieved and accomplished so much by my early thirties. I am a first-generation college student, the first doctora in my family, and a successful business owner. And while it can be challenging to give myself the title of "Change Maker," I realize I have undoubtedly broken generational chains and am stepping, poco-a-poco, into my power as a strong, unapologetic Latina who carries herself with confidence and grace.

As I reflect on my journey and my experiences, I recognize the importance of understanding one's own narrative and how it shapes our present and future. This introspective process mirrors the approach I take professionally as a clinical psychologist, where the foundation of my work lies in deeply comprehending the personal stories of those I serve.

One of the first conversations I have with prospective therapy clients is about how I want to get to know and better understand the person sitting in front of me. I want to learn how the individual is shaped by their own unique experiences and life circumstances that have made them "them." By exploring and honoring our backgrounds and experiences, both in my personal life and through my therapeutic practice, I strive to facilitate a deeper connection and growth in these relationships. This holistic understanding not only enriches my own journey but also empowers me to support others in navigating their paths with insight and empathy. One of those roads I routinely walk with my BIPOC clients is exploring their own cultural identities and how they intersect, guiding familiar conversations I have had myself.

My Latinidad is one identity that has always been present in my life, but my relationship with mi cultura and mis raices has grown and evolved over time. As a kid, I never thought of my Latinx identity as overly salient, largely because I grew up in a smaller agricultural town where most of us looked alike and grew up together in our community. I also had a large extended family that we joked made up most of our small town. To me, being Latina and part of a large Mexican family was so obviously part of my day-to-day. It was not until I left for college that I started to think more curiously about what it meant to be "Latina."

Removing myself from a small community meant I had to step outside my comfort zone and take on new challenges, such as adapting to more autonomy and discovering different aspects of myself. For as long as I can remember, I was academically driven and understood I would one day leave my hometown to attend college. My parents continually exemplified a strong work ethic that I strived to achieve throughout my youth and to this day. My parents, who were small agricultural business owners and had not gone to college, instilled in me a determination to focus on my studies so that I could successfully venture out of our community. As the oldest of three siblings, I was the first to go to college, and eventually the first to pursue a graduate degree. Leaving my small town was a scary, yet worthwhile experience. As part of that journey, my Latina identity became more prominent, and I reestablished how to honor this part of my identity when I was in spaces with others who looked less like me.

When I think about what it means for me to be "Latina," and to achieve the level of success I have achieved in life, I have to give significant credit to the women in my family. I come from a family of really strong mujeres, including my mother, grandmothers, tias, and cousins. I admit my bias when I say this, but I believe the women hold my family down. My family is generally very traditional when it comes to gender roles, and the women are typically the ones cooking, plating, and serving their husbands' meals, while taking care of the home and children. Without us women, our men would not know what to do with themselves. I know I am speaking in large generalizations, but I often tell my dad he could not survive without my mom. Sorry, Dad.

But the women who come to mind when I think about strong mujeres in my family are my grandmothers, my "Grandma" and my "Nana." I lost both sooner than I ever imagined I would, but their spirits live on within me. My Nana, my maternal grandmother, passed away unexpectedly when I was in the fourth grade. She was my first experience with death and grief and as you can imagine, I was not ready. I still vividly remember the day I broke down crying after her funeral because her home which was filled with positive memories would no longer be the same after we lost the matriarch of our family. My senior year of high school, in my AP English class, I was required to write a series of essays, which I dedicated to my Nana, and wrote several entries about how she influenced my upbringing and psychological and moral growth. My mom still has this book, sitting alongside my doctoral dissertation, which I guess is funny of me to think I was not already an author, but I digress. In one of the entries, I wrote:

"I was in the fourth grade the year I realized people I know could die. In my mind, I know other people, strangers, died, but I was unaware that anyone who meant something special to me could be affected in such a way."

In my reflections, I recognize how impactful my early experiences with grief shaped my upbringing and my life experiences that followed. I thought of my Nana often as I progressed in school, graduated from middle school and then high school, and so on and so forth, wishing she could see everything I accomplished and the woman I was becoming. I grieved the moments she was not there during difficult times when I would have loved a hug or a home-cooked comfort meal from her. My Grandma, my paternal grandmother, later passed away during my senior year of college before she could see me graduate from the University of California, Berkeley. My Grandma was sick for approximately two years, so while it was more "expected," it did not hurt any less. Naturally, I remember my Grandma's hugs a little bit better. Her embrace was so strong until the end, and I can still feel her arms around me now. Both of my grandmothers passed away during transitional periods in my life, and it was a strange experience to feel both excitement and grief during those times without these women present. It was a heavy, significant impact when I lost my Nana, but the hole was left even more agape when I lost my Grandma too.

I remember my grandmothers often in every new challenge or opportunity I come across, and I view them as my guardian angels who are always whispering encouraging messages into my ear. I wear a sapphire ring I inherited from my Nana, with whom I share the same birthstone, as a small reminder that I am strong, capable, and competent, and I always have my guardian angels around me.

As I grew older, I learned more about each of my grandmothers, and it was continuously very clear they separately endured multiple hardships in their lives. From growing up impoverished in Mexico to immigrating to the United States and settling in Monterey County, California, to working long, arduous hours in the carrot and garlic packing sheds. They both had husbands, my grandfathers, who embodied the stereotypical machismo attitude and treated them as subordinates. Additionally, my Grandma, at approximately age 60, learned her husband secretly had a separate second family, my father's half-siblings, and went on to later divorce him. This latter experience I have learned is something far too common within our culture as well.

My grandmothers were not given very many opportunities in life to be more than mothers and wives, and I was never afforded the opportunity to ask them if they had ever dreamt of more than that for themselves. What I do know is my grandmothers were proud of me, and I feel very lucky and blessed to be one of the oldest grandchildren on both sides who had the most time with each of them. I do my best to honor them by finding ways to feel more rooted in my Mexican heritage, whether that is by maintaining my Spanish proficiency, trying to do justice to their cooking recipes, including tamales with my mom during the Christmas season, and speaking their names and their stories to my younger brothers and cousins, and one day, my future children.

As a licensed clinical psychologist, I am educated in generational trauma and speak often of it during my therapy sessions with clients. In short, generational trauma is the transmission of traumatic experiences or stressors that are passed down from one generation to the next. Although we are exposed to our families' historical traumas, such as the negative experiences and burdens my grandmothers carried, I realize I also received my resilience and empathy from them. I was blessed to receive both my perseverance and natural listening skills from them as well. These are all gifts they gave me, ones I hold onto and that ground me in those moments when I wish they were physically still on this earth.

At the same time, it would be remiss of me to not acknowledge that sometimes it can be exhausting to be a change maker, breaking generational chains and unloading burdens, battling imposter syndrome, establishing healthy boundaries with yourself and/or others, and all the other things you may or may not be working through. So, it is essential, required even, to build up your self-care regimen. In addition to those enjoyable activities that come to mind when you think of self-care, I encourage you to find somewhere or someone who brings you calmness and tranquility. Maybe that is a location, a loved one, a specific mindset or image, or a combination of all three. For me, my place of grounding is by the ocean, listening to the sounds of waves, or through movement, such as running. Maybe it looks different for you, or you are still figuring it out. That's okay! I just want to encourage you to give yourself permission to rest and restore your energy. You are not the burdens you carry. We have to keep going and rising.

In the therapy setting, I often educate and encourage my clients to recognize two polarizing thoughts or feelings can coexist and be "true" at the same time. For example, I shared I experienced two opposing feelings during transitional seasons in my life, where I felt excited about my accomplishments but also sad with the absence of my grandmothers. Given these were periods in my life before attending graduate school, I did not fully understand that these two conflicting feelings could coexist at the same time, but this is something I learned and applied to myself early in my training and remind myself of often.

As humans when we experience two emotions that feel incompatible, sometimes we start to feel a third emotion, "guilt." We may experience guilt for feeling happy, joyful, or successful, when we are also sad, grieving, or realize we were afforded opportunities that our previous generations did not have. While something can be terrifying and scary because it is unfamiliar or the outcome is uncertain, it can bring us immense pride and delight to turn a dream or goal into reality. When I look back over time, I realize I have had multiple experiences that were both anxiety-inducing and thrilling at the same time: When I left home to pursue my undergraduate degree at

UC Berkeley, when I studied abroad in a foreign country, when I changed my mind about my major about five times, when I chose to pursue my doctorate degree at Palo Alto University, and when I took a leap of faith to leave my stable "agency" job to establish my own psychological private practice.

As I write this, I catch myself only bringing up my academic or career-driven decisions because those are commonly where these emotions arise. When thinking about the title of "Latinas Rising," I feel compelled to highlight my successes and reinforce my credibility. However, it is important to show this dialectical thinking pattern can be, and is often, applied to our most personal stressors and achievements as well. Here are some of mine: When I chose to end relationships that were no longer serving me or bringing me joy, when I recently chose to take an opportunity to travel to a foreign country alone, when I chose to run a marathon, when I chose to start therapy (*we love a therapist who does her own therapy*), and when I chose to prioritize the relationship I have with myself versus caring more about the ones I have with others. All these decisions, both personally and professionally, came con miedo pero con mucho orgullo. I hope you find yourself reflecting and identifying your own experiences that have brought you these emotions too.

I could not possibly end my story without encouraging you to try therapy if you have not done so already. The therapy environment is such a wonderful space for embarking on self-exploration, navigating a transitional period, or processing cultural identities, self-esteem, boundary issues, and so much more. It is even more rewarding and transformative when you find the right therapist "fit" for you. Interested in starting therapy? You can start here: Latinx Therapy (www.latinxtherapy.com). This is an amazing directory, full of Latinx therapists across the United States, and you can filter out based on your criteria.

Therapy is a space to unapologetically be your authentic self. One of the best parts for me as a clinical psychologist is helping other Latinas realize their full potential and embrace who they are meant to be. I have the privilege of observing this growth and change happen in my clients, and I do not take that for granted. What has brought me the most success in my private practice and maintaining this privilege of witnessing clients' growth in their therapy journeys, is my resolve to show up as my authentic self.

There is an older school of thought in which mental health professionals are taught and encouraged to remain a "blank canvas" and not introduce parts of themselves into the therapy session. Indeed, there are specific institutional settings where I would exercise caution with self-disclosure. However, I believe tactfully using self-disclosure in community settings and in private practice with BIPOC folx strengthens my therapeutic reach. For each session with my clients, I pledge to help them unload their burdens and provide a space to explore stressors with compassion and strength. At the end of the day, I strive to maintain a safe, nonjudgmental space to help others find the change they are seeking. In a similar fashion, my hope is that readers of this book become their own change makers, discover and embrace their self-worth, and understand their significance within their communities and the broader world.

ABOUT DR. MARISSA VASQUEZ

Dr. Marissa Vasquez is a third-generation Mexican American who was born and raised in Monterey County, California. She is a first-generation college student and the first in her family to pursue a doctorate degree. She received her PhD in Clinical Psychology from Palo Alto University in 2020 and is now a licensed clinical psychologist serving California residents across the state virtually and in-person at her office in Pacific Grove. In her free time, she enjoys spending time with her family and friends, her soul dog, Penny, and being outdoors, hiking, or reading a good book.

Website: www.vasquezpsychservices.com

13
NIKKI STORMS

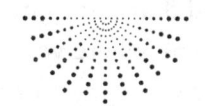

I **work in human resources. Culture and inclusion to be specific.** It's not a career path most would think of as exciting. It probably wasn't in your top five dream jobs. I've come to realize though; it is a career that surprisingly gets me a ton of questions about how I got to be in this line of work...right after I explain to people what exactly it is.

Honestly, I'm still just as surprised as most are when they hear that I got my degree in Art History and had a very bright future in museum and gallery work in my early twenties. I was also on a pretty damn good trajectory in my marketing career right after I left the art world.

The truth is. This work wasn't my original plan. It wasn't something I dreamed of as a kid, in fact, it never even crossed my mind. I got here because I took a chance (a pretty big one) and followed my heart.

So, how did this Latina rise to the occasion? It's kind of a long story. Or rather a few short stories.

I walked out of THAT meeting feeling absolutely gutted. Defeated.

Many of us have had THAT meeting. You know, the one that ends up being a pivotal moment in your career. The one that you left furious. The one where you left early for the day because you weren't going to be productive after it. The one where you went over your family budget in your head, to figure out if there was a way you could just quit and leave today. The one where you are thankful you maintained your composure and didn't say out loud, the things you were saying in your head. The one where you question why you've ever worked as hard as you have. The one where you question all your professional decisions. The one where you doubt yourself. The one where you almost cried. The one where...ok, you did cry a little—but you weren't going to let them see you cry. You know. THAT meeting.

I had expected it to be a standard annual review meeting. I loved my boss. They knew me, cared about me, my family, and my career development. Having that kind of support helped me grow and become better in my job and with my team. I wanted to make a difference. In my work. For the company. With my team. I wanted to help drive results, because I knew my team and I could. We were innovators. We embraced technology, looked for new and efficient ways of doing work and we were committed to tracking our results.

So, when I walked into THAT meeting and saw that a more senior leader was also joining my manager and me, I was...curious. It wasn't how these meetings typically went.

I was grateful and thrilled to hear from my manager that I was getting a positive review and that I was also receiving a promotion, with an increase in salary and a promoted title. Yes! My hard work was paying off.

It was when that third voice in the room finished the conversation that things took a turn I never would have imagined. Especially the impact it ended up having on me.

"You are too aggressive... too outspoken... I almost reconsidered giving you this promotion..." I blacked out a little bit after that.

That was it. That's all it took. A few words and my spirit was broken. I tried not to let them see it, but I was left confused. There was no way I was even in the top 50 of people whom I worked with that I would consider as aggressive or most outspoken.

I couldn't help but think, "Am I not allowed to be outspoken? What is wrong with being outspoken, or honest and forthright?"

I knew I didn't fit the mold. I didn't look like the other leaders in this group. I knew I was newer to this group, and younger. I knew I was challenging how things were typically done. I knew my ideas, or maybe my style, didn't bode well with some.

I wondered to myself, "Do I become aggressive when I feel I'm not being heard?"

I couldn't stop thinking about these words that stuck with me or the way I felt in the aftermath of this conversation. I'm sure this leader didn't intend to strike this chord in me and certainly not this deeply. This wasn't a malicious person. They probably moved on with their day and didn't realize I was left questioning my professional purpose. This conversation was probably never even given a second thought.

Meanwhile, this situation left me feeling like I didn't fit in. I didn't fit into the culture. I wasn't allowed to show up as opinionated, driven, or ambitious. I told myself that those were traits that were reserved for others, not those like me.

I felt like I was left with two choices. Stay and do the work in a way that wasn't authentically me, with my ambition and drive dimmed. Or leave.

I couldn't help but dwell on how this conversation left me feeling. I spent many of my days after, thinking about it, trying to figure out why I felt the way I did - what had triggered me and why. I began to examine two personal experiences in my life that have significantly influenced my values, beliefs, and behaviors.

～

"One day, you will regret that you never wanted to learn Spanish."

I heard this phrase over a thousand times growing up. It wasn't that I didn't want to learn—I was adamant that I didn't need to learn it. This is America after all. What good will it do me? We speak English here. Everyone around me spoke English...well, mostly.

English was the only language my sisters and I knew, despite Spanish being spoken around us when we visited our Mexican side of the family. It was my grandparents' first language, so it was normal to me that I didn't always understand what the adults on that side of the family were saying.

When my mom spoke to her parents, siblings, and cousins, they would switch from English to Spanish when they would gossip or say stuff they didn't want the kids to hear. It just seemed like a secret code language that they had so, I brushed Spanish off as something I didn't need to know, maybe even I shouldn't know.

At six, I realized that my mom was probably the only person in our town who spoke Spanish. I would get so embarrassed when she would speak it under her breath at the store when she was annoyed with someone. Growing up in a small, rural-at-the-time, town outside of Des Moines, I knew my mom was the only Hispanic person in our town. To be clear, she was the only person of color in the town.

I would always specify that my sisters and I were half-Mexican, half-white. I didn't see us as the same as my mom, which drove her nuts. I think it even hurt her. In her mind, since she was Mexican...so were we. Looking back, I still don't agree with her. Yes, I am Hispanic, a Latina—I am Mexican. ...and I'm also white. My dad was white. I can't agree that I'm one without the other—I'm both. My life experience was different than hers. It was also vastly different from my dad's.

I spent many of my younger years going to Sunday mass in Spanish. We celebrated Christmas Eve by making tamales with our tias and female cousins. We'd go to the Mexican dances on weekends, where I and all the other kids would fall asleep on folding chairs while the adults danced to banda all night. I admired the quinceneras, helped make homemade tortillas, petted the goats my grandpa would butcher to make birria, ate all the pan dulce and limon y tajin candies from the tienda, beat pinatas with a broomstick at every birthday, and I'm able to say all these words in a fairly accurate Spanish accent.

I also got to experience racism-a-plenty as a kid. I heard Mexican jokes and black jokes (kids often didn't know what race I was, being a dark-skinned kid) and was assured they "didn't mean you." I was asked if I was legal and if my family was illegal. I was told to "go back where I came from" (hello, born here). Kids joked that my family would be deported. I was called racial slurs, of all sorts, not just related to Hispanics and Latinos. Today I'm still often asked, "What are you?."

One of my fondest childhood racism memories was at the park across the street from our house. We played there often, but this one afternoon, some random kids that we had never seen there before were on the equipment. While sharing the playground, my sisters and I were asked what we were (again). After replying "Mexican," the kids asked us if we had knives—insinuating that all Mexicans, even kids apparently, are dangerous and carry knives. A close contender to my favorite childhood racist moment was when my oldest sister was called a "spic" by her sixth-grade teacher...who went on to become an elementary principal in the district.

I learned early on in life that being Mexican was not considered as great of a thing to everyone, as my mom told me it was. As a small child, I wondered if maybe it was better to be white. At one point I started telling my Mexican cousins, tias, and tios that I didn't want to be Mexican—I was white. A memory that one of my tios reminded me of in my early twenties, and not for a laugh but for shame's sake. (We were never particularly close with this tio). Nothing like throwing my childhood trauma in my face.

The irony is that from time to time, my sisters and I were occasionally teased and called "güeras," white girls, by our cousins and tias and tios. We were often reminded that we weren't full-blooded

Mexicans. We were sometimes teased for living in a white town—because that made us "act white."

So, as my community made it abundantly clear that I didn't belong as a Mexican girl—there were times when I definitely didn't feel like I fit in on my Mexican family's side either, as a half-white girl.

I've never fit into any one culture. Maybe I never would.

∼

My mom was always sick.

I was used to saying my mom was disabled but I don't think I ever really grasped what that meant. Her pain was non-apparent. There were no injuries or accidents or root causes that anyone could easily see or point to.

She had a job in my early childhood, it was the mid-eighties. I was around three or four when she was working in operations for a publishing company. The timeline is fuzzy, but I went to a daycare facility at one point and my maternal (Mexican) grandma, Josephina, watched me at times.

I loved being with my grandma. We watched The Price is Right, then her soaps came on and she'd let me watch Flintstones and the Jetsons in the afternoon. Most days were pretty chill at the house since she didn't drive.

Sometimes, Grandma and I would take little bus trips around Des Moines—usually to her doctor appointments at the hospital. She struggled with diabetes, specifically with kidney health. A regular trip we'd take was to pick up their commodity foods. This was before SNAP or EBT cards. In short, if you were poor, you would go to a local commodity food center and pick up basic "healthy" foods. In the eighties, this consisted of boxes of powdered milk, cans of fruit and fruit juice, boxes of raisins, grainy peanut butter (which I actually really loved), and God-awful processed cheese, among other things. I ate what my grandparents had and a lot of times if it wasn't the authentic Mexican food my grandpa made, it was this.

Soon enough, my days at daycare and at Grandma's came to an end. Mom had to stop working and I stayed home with her. Her pain became too frequent and attending work regularly was not possible.

In the next few proceeding years, I made more trips to the hospital, but these were for Mom's regular doctor appointments and numerous hospitalizations. Once, our family took a drive up to the Mayo Clinic in Minnesota, where Mom had a number of tests to figure out why she wasn't walking due to a mysterious pain. Previous diagnoses were arthritis, but that trip earned her a new diagnosis of Raynaud's.

The pain in her legs was so severe at times, that she would be admitted to the hospital for a spinal block to numb the lower half of her body. My sisters and I eventually knew our way around all Des Moines-area hospitals, including all the nurse's stations that were stocked up on little cartons of orange sherbet and soda. When a McDonald's opened in one of the hospitals, our minds were blown.

We were just kids and didn't understand the severity of our mom's condition. She would be fine one day, and the next she could be in tears, begging for the pain to go away. Her spinal blocks became so commonplace that it seemed as normal as getting a flu shot. Eventually, she did endure a mis-administered block that resulted in a collapsed lung. Over her lifetime, she would have had so many spinal blocks, that the real risk had become accidental paralysis due to the amount of scar tissue she had developed in her spine and so doctors would no longer offer these as an option to manage her pain.

In the early nineties, Mom earned a new neurological diagnosis: Reflex Sympathetic Dystrophy, now called Complex Regional Pain Syndrome. When I was in fourth grade, there was a period when she couldn't walk for about three months because the burning pain in her legs wouldn't go away. She would lay in bed, crying from the constant pain. She eventually had to move into a rehabilitation center so that she could be taught how to live with the pain and get around in a wheelchair.

Can you imagine? Being taught to live your life around that kind of pain. They taught her how to get around a kitchen and how to cook while in a wheelchair, while in this intense pain.

A new narcotic came on the market and Oxycontin barged into our family. Mom had been on various types of pharmaceuticals throughout her disability journey, in an attempt to ease the pain her own body had created. Nothing worked. Oxy was promoted as this miracle drug that would allow her to have her life back. The contrary became her truth. In fact, it seemed to suck life out of all of us.

There was a significant period through the nineties to the early 2000s when mom's addiction to Oxycontin was central to our everyday life. There were days she would seem ok, but that would quickly take a turn to her being in a zombie state, falling asleep while standing as she would put a load of laundry in.

Often, I'd walk into the living room, and she'd be passed out with food hanging half out of her mouth. She had passed out mid-bite. We'd find burn marks on blankets, chairs, sofas, side tables, the carpet, and even on her bedspread, from cigarette cherries that would fall when she passed out while smoking in the house.

Despite any of her close calls with fire while passed out from the drug, the worst moment by far was when I was a sophomore or junior in high school. I had just gotten home from school when the phone rang. It was the Iowa State Highway Patrol asking for my dad.

Mom had been in a car accident on the interstate. She passed out while driving to a doctor's appointment. It was believed that the only reason she was still alive from the crash was because she was driving my dad's prized possession, his 1960s Dodge Coronet. He had just recently restored this car from top to bottom. It was now totaled, and Mom was in the hospital, followed up by drug detox and rehab.

During these years, the "professionals" deemed drug addiction on Oxy as not the drug's fault, or even the prescriber's fault, and it certainly was no fault of the pharmaceutical company. It was deemed user abuse.

Over the years, Mom struggled with continued overuse of the highly addictive drug and bouts of depression. She'd be in tears often, crying for the pain to go away. Crying for it to end. Desperation and sorrow seemed to represent the person she had become.

My mom believed in Mexican curanderos and sought their help for her healing. At an early age, I had heard stories from my mom, tias, and cousins about brujas that put evil spells on people that did wrong to them or their families. These were tales of sickness and hauntings. Was it Mexican Folklorico or was it real? I never really knew. It was real enough to me because I learned it as a part of my culture. But even the curanderos didn't work for her.

Mom was eventually able to leave Oxy and methadone behind her and found relief in other pain relief options that didn't take her life away. But she did pass away too young, just like her mom did, barely at sixty. Her body had had enough.

My mom wasn't like the moms my friends had. She usually couldn't do the things other moms did. She couldn't have a career. She grew up poor and our own family struggled financially. I wonder if she had hopes, dreams, or goals for herself or if the despair of her health won every time.

I always told myself that I would never be like my mom. I didn't want to be hopeless. I set many dreams and goals for myself and was hell-bent to make them happen. She couldn't do it, but I would, and I would work my ass off to do it.

I would be focused and determined with a drive and work ethic that was unmatched.

∼

What I eventually realized after THAT meeting, was that I had a third choice.

I decided to take a path that led me to workforce relational development. I want to prevent others from feeling how I felt after THAT meeting. I want to create environments that help people feel understood, accepted, and valued for being themselves.

I realized that the leader didn't really know me. Perhaps they had an idea of who they wanted me to be like though. Sometimes leaders can do that, I've been guilty of it too. Like parents, they concoct a vision of how people should behave or perform. It's bias at its finest.

Ultimately—I am me because of my lived experiences and I don't want to feel shame or feel I need to conform to be like anyone else. Nor do I want anyone else to feel those things. We can be successful by being who we are. The workplace shouldn't be about fitting into a culture, it should be about evolving it. A healthy workplace culture understands and invites people to bring their own uniquely special lives, experiences, and talents into it.

So, I found a career in culture and inclusion. I am an advocate for everyone to feel acceptance and to give mutual respect. This means not leaving your personal stuff at the door, but inviting it in.

Perhaps it was divine intervention or maybe it was destiny that an opportunity arose. I may never know. But this Latina rose to the occasion and took a chance—on herself too. I intend to keep rising and hope to bring others along with me.

ABOUT NIKKI STORMS

Nikki Storms is a mixed-race Latina from Kansas City, Missouri. Originally from a small, rural town in Iowa, Nikki studied Art, Art History, and Entrepreneurship at the University of Iowa. After a short stint working in museums and art galleries, she created a career for herself in marketing and communications. During the pandemic years, she pondered her personal passions and turned to a new career in workforce relations, specifically culture and inclusion, and a new hobby of writing.

When she's not writing, Nikki enjoys regularly chatting with her sisters, nieces, and nephews in their family group text and spending time with her own family including her husband and high-school sweetheart, and three kids. She can usually be found on the sidelines of a youth sporting event or driving to one.

Website: www.midlifemamacita.com
LinkedIn: www.linkedin.com/in/nikki-storms
Email: nleestorms@gmail.com

14
PATTY SAMUDIO

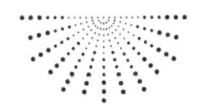

I'm living my best life... or at least I'm really trying to. I'm on a journey of reflection, healing, forgiveness, and acceptance. I wanted to one day share my stories when I was done with my journey, but this is a never-ending process as I continue to heal, grow, and evolve. I have already been taken through many peaks and valleys and there are many more I will travel through because my life is one big journey. This is my story.

My father was born and raised in southern California. He was the 4th of 6 children, his mother died during the labor of her sixth child when my father was about 3.5 years old. He ended up in prison for a brief time. While there he learned how to cook, and he would use this skill later in life. He escaped prison and went across the border to lay low for a while and that is where he would eventually cross paths with my mother.

My mother was born and raised in Michoacan, Mexico. She was the oldest of eleven children. Her mother was a homemaker who tended to her home and children along with my mom. They lived a very humble and hard life that didn't include much of an education for my mom. After all, during her childhood era if there was any money for education that would go to sending one of her brothers to school as it was viewed as a waste of money to send a daughter, especially if there was no money. It was her duty as a daughter and as the oldest to stay home and help her mother tend to the household chores, cooking, and caring for her younger siblings.

My parents were married in Old Mesilla, New Mexico, on November 12, 1963. Their marriage didn't start on a solid foundation and was set up to fail. They were not raised from a similar background or upbringing. The old Mexican traditional ways my mother was raised were so different from the Southern California ways my father was raised so they rarely saw eye to eye on anything. My father worked as a professional chef and my mother a homemaker. They became parents to five daughters, from oldest to the youngest there is an 11-year age gap. I am the 4th child, the second youngest.

I say this with great love and respect for both my parents but neither knew how to be parents, but they didn't exactly have the right model to follow either, it was a different era, and things were done differently back then. I think that era started to end, and a new era started 10-11 years into their marriage when separation and divorce weren't as scandalous as everyone made them out to be. There's no doubt that both loved me and my sisters, but each had their faults. My father spoiled us, there was never any real discipline from him that I can recall, and he undermined my mother's parenting in front of us girls. My mother wanted to raise us in the very traditional strict way she was raised in Mexico, which wasn't appeasing to my father, and she could be disrespectful towards my father in front of us girls.

Their parenting approaches were constantly clashing which led to many arguments, eventually separation, and very confused children. My father died on February 24, 1983, but by this time their inability to compromise, communicate, and parent/co-parent had its consequences with all of us girls, each of us in very different lasting ways. My mom was left with five girls to raise, barely speaking any English, no education, and at this point she never fully assimilated.

I have experienced all types of abuse, but I would like to preface that the physical and sexual abuse I endured was not at the hands of either parent. For as long as I can remember I was constantly told I was ugly, unlovable, no man would ever marry me or want to be with me. I was told many times by one of my Tia's in her joking, nicest, "aww I feel sorry for you" kind of way that men were only going to use me to get what they wanted or use me to get closer to my more beautiful sisters. One of my sisters would remind me that if she wanted, she could take any boy she wanted away from me. I was reminded that I needed to keep my nose in the books because I would have to not only take care of myself, but I would have to take care of my mom since my sisters would be busy raising their families.

The physical abuse came from one of my older sisters. She groomed me from a young age to never speak about it and I lived in fear the next beating would be worse. I honestly don't know if she even realized what she was doing or the consequences of her actions because she was a teenager. Another older sister was an instigator, she would go to the other sister and tell her God knows what to infuriate her and I would get another beating, be tormented, or both. I refer to my childhood home as the house of horrors, most don't understand because they thought coming to our house was fun or it was cool to hang out with some of my sisters and the friends that would gather there. Imagine being asleep for the night and waking up to your sister straddling you and beating you out of your sleep, it was not fun for me.

There was an incident when my mom and dad were separated, and my mom left for Mexico for a month. Instead of allowing us to stay with my dad, she had her brother, his girlfriend, and their toddler come to stay with us. My uncle's toddler put a bristle brush in his mouth and my little sister who was 5 years old at the time tried getting it from him. The bristle brush ended up cutting the inside of his mouth which bled, and he belted out a scream. When my uncle went to investigate, and he saw his son bleeding without hesitation he took off his belt and started beating my little sister with it. She ended up black and blue and he managed to break skin because he was hitting her with the buckle portion.

To say the incident was traumatizing isn't even the half of it. That incident is so etched into my brain, my memories, and my body that to this day my anxiety goes through the roof when I hear a scream/cry for help from a child. We were taken away and placed in a receiving home and not allowed to be taken home by my dad, this was before his death, as they were also trying to locate my mom who was in Mexico with family who had no phone before a judge would decide what to do with us. We were separated by our age and weren't allowed to stay together.

It was at this receiving home that I first felt my body violated. I remember putting up a fight when it came time to shower because I was too young to shower myself according to their policy. The shower was an accessible area, there was a stranger not only seeing me naked but touching me unclothed as random people walked by for all to see. It was a traumatizing, horrifying, and humiliating experience for 7-year-old me. When we were allowed to spend time together, ironically, I felt safe because my sisters were familiar within this strange place. When our visits were over, and we had to go back to our assigned areas, the feeling of dread would wash over me. Having to leave my little sister behind in the oversized jailed crib that they kept her in haunts me and her screams and cries as we left have never left me.

I was almost 9 years old when a church member began molesting me. By this time, my dad had passed away and my mom was working multiple jobs to make ends meet. I think during this time my mom felt it was unsafe to leave me and my younger sister at home with our older sisters. My mom was friends with my abuser and his wife, and I was friends with their children. This man was a predator and he recognized that there were vulnerabilities within our family, and he took advantage of those vulnerabilities. He recognized that I was already groomed to keep my mouth shut and pretend everything was fine.

He used his children as excuses to get me and my little sister to come over and play with his children and of course to help my mom out so she would have peace of mind that we were safe with a church family while she worked. I did nothing to protect myself because I had no self-worth, I was unlovable and felt I deserved this, this is what I was made for, or so the events of my life up to that point led me to believe. My self-worth was taken from me many years ago by my sister. Now the little piece of innocence I had left my abuser took away from me.

I was 10 years old when a girl around my age helped me escape from him, she too was a prior victim. We were at a public pool, and we were surrounded by adults but not one adult was paying any attention. I was so thankful that someone, even someone as young as her, finally came to my rescue. The bad thing was my little sister was with me and he went to her to try and do the same to her as he had been doing to me for months. Up until that point, I was able to steer him away from her by using myself as a shield to protect her. At the pool, I knew I was no match for him but there was no way I was going to let him hurt my little sister. I grabbed my little sister by the hand and forced her out of the public pool, boy was she angry with me, and we went straight to my mom. The only reason I finally spoke up and told my mom everything was to protect my little sister, never for myself. Fortunately, she never took us to spend time with that man and his family again.

Unfortunately, my mom told me to forget whatever happened and never speak of it. She told me if I did that, they would take us away from her again and this time they would keep us, and we would be separated from her permanently. Unlike the last time when we were taken and released into my dad's custody, this time my dad was dead. I still vividly remember the first experience at the receiving home so there was no way I was going to say anything and go back to that place. I repressed the experience as much as I could, but those types of experiences have a way of catching up to you.

Not long after this, I began secretly drinking. My father's liquor was still in the cabinet above the fridge and my mom rarely drank. I needed to do something to numb the pain, so I started mixing the alcohol in my Kool-Aid. As I would get closer to drinking up the bottle, I would fill them with Kool-Aid or water, so they still looked full. Nobody was none the wiser for a long time, eventually my mom suspected but she always suspected the wrong daughter. Throughout high school and a few years after high school, I smoked marijuana and eventually harder drugs. Alcohol alone was no longer giving me that numbing effect that I desperately wanted. I always had one leg on each side of the fence but so many people were unaware or just did not notice, after all, they had their own problems.

Throughout my life from childhood to the present day and all the traumatizing experiences I've had I always felt close to God. He has been with me and by my side through all of it. He has put some very amazing people in my path who have shown me love, acceptance, and compassion, provided me with sound advice, and just good-hearted people. It amazes me at times that I'm still alive, that I'm not a drug addict or alcoholic. I'm relatively healthy, I'm going to therapy to help me learn to heal from my past and try my best every day to be a better person and learn to trust people. I never thought in a million years I would be sharing my past life in hopes of helping one person by writing a chapter in a book.

I am a divorcee and I've been a single mother, for about 18 years, to two beautiful children. My daughter is studying in the medical field and my son is a Marine reservist and works in a warehouse. My motivation to break the chain and change my life started with my daughter. I looked into her eyes and knew I wanted a better life for her. It was up to me to break the cycle with my children. I did my best to do exactly that, and I hope it was enough so they could carry that mindset with their own children.

I raised them to have all the opportunities I didn't have. I raised them with love and guidance, I pushed education, I made them follow through on their commitments, to try new things, to keep an open mind, and provided them with the tools I didn't get. I allowed them to see me fail, they knew my past, and I never lied to them about that or kept it a secret. They've seen me work hard, take care of my mother when she suffered from Alzheimer's, they experienced all the struggles with me when their father and I divorced, and they supported me when I went back to school to get my AS degree so I could continue to advance in my career. I work for the state and not only am I a Latina in the IT field but I'm also in management.

When I started there weren't many women in the IT field let alone many Latinas, the IT field was known as the good ol' boys club. This meant I had to work extra hard, keep up with the changing technologies, and not let anyone challenging me or trying to set me up to fail to get the best of me. At times, I was the only female in the room with no allies. No matter, I kept my head up, stayed focused, and persevered through it all. This past year, after 23 years in the IT field, it is the first time I've come across another Latina in management in a higher classification than me, que orgullo. We are so few and far between and I'm damn proud of being part of this very small but mighty group of women. I hope from this point on there will be so many other young Latinas joining the ranks.

I gave you a glimpse into my life and didn't dig deeper into my loving but complicated relationship with my mother. There was so much more that transpired that could have taken me down and destroyed me, but I could never cover it all in one chapter. I know there will be some who my story will resonate with, and with others, it will not. For those with similar experiences to mine I say to you, take control of your life and live it exactly the way you want. You don't have to stop dreaming and desiring a better life. You can live it, there is no limit, only the limit you put on yourself.

I turned my experiences from a negative to a positive because I knew I didn't want, for me or my children, to stay a victim and live a victim's life. I wanted to be a survivor and a champion for those with similar experiences. I still have plenty of healing to be done, I honestly haven't been on this path alone. Like I said, God put some amazing people in my path. Look for your people, surround yourself with people who will be supportive of you, who want better for you, who uplift you, and should you fall, they will reach down and pull you up and never leave you behind. Continue or begin your journey of self-healing, self-love, and continue to evolve and grow. Be the change-maker in someone's life.

I have mentored others in the IT career path, my fellow Latinos, people of color, and especially my Latinas. Every time I get the chance I will speak with the younger generation in my family and their friends about the importance of education, and of living a different life than the ones dictated by the neighborhoods we grew up in. The time is now for us to stop being silent. Let our stories be heard, let the healing and growth begin, and be the change makers that we were always meant to be.

We don't have to be victims of our experiences, we don't have to live our parents' lives, we don't have to live how our culture or traditions dictate, we don't have to be statistics, and we don't have to limit our dreams and desires. Live your best life!

ABOUT PATTY SAMUDIO

Patty Samudio started her career for the state as a student assistant and has worked her way up to Information Technology Management. When given the opportunity she speaks to the younger generation about the importance of education, careers in the IT field, and making their dreams a reality. She aspires to be a positive influence on her family, Latinos, the younger generation, and anyone with similar experiences as her.

Patty is a proud mother of a daughter who is studying in the medical field and a son who is a Marine Reservist and warehouse worker. She loves to travel and is planning to travel the world to see all the beauty God created.

15
YG COLLABORATIONS

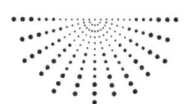

Y & G COLLABORATE: THE CRAZY TRAIN CONNECTION

The beaming sun was beginning to peak, and flowing white polyester fabric hung from the wooden trellis without a hint of any breeze. Our soon-to-arrive guests had no idea they were about to become bacon in the sun and the appetizers for a hive of lovebugs. The irony of a swarm of aggressive and vibrant lovebugs at an outdoor ceremony site attacking the wedding decor was humorous for about two seconds. We paced quickly from inside to outside the venue, opening perfectly placed wooden chairs while muttering frustration over the un-mowed grass that made it hard to set the chairs evenly.

We were rolling along at full speed when we came to a screeching halt. "What are we doing?" I asked Geo as sweat dripped down every part of my body, even in places I didn't know could sweat. I remember her giving me the usual *"What do you mean, what are we doing?"* look on her face as she continued to place the white fabric. "Why are we out here sweating to death, parched, feet tingling from the heat, needing a shower and new clothes?" she replied light-heartedly. I was dead serious. I sat on a nearby swing and asked the question again. "What are we doing?" I said. "I don't know," she said slowly, which is not her usual cadence. She hopped on the swing beside me and, for a few minutes, we just paused. We had no idea how bad our need to pause was. How taking a long breath would open our inner thoughts and dreams to the choices ahead. Our subconscious creativity and aspirations felt woven together in this pausing moment. Coincidental yet destined to intersect.

Geo and I had met before this hot day from hell, back when someone mentioned the pressing need to join the both of us. They were not wrong; we are grateful to have been connected at the right time. I knew a kindred spirit connection had transpired in our first casual conversation. When I got back in my car, I said, "What just happened?" Do you know when you meet someone, and you already have a sense that you know them? It is a sense of recognition that transcends time, as if they had crossed your path or were perhaps a missing piece of a grand puzzle. It is always the one piece in the puzzle that clarifies how the whole thing begins to take shape. I was not a very trusting person for years in an industry that granted awards to the most self-seeking individuals. The synergy between us was vibrant enough to catch our attention, and a hint of a familiar bond opened the door to curiosity.

Geo felt the same familiar joint connection and she contacted me shortly after that encounter to see if I wanted to help her find new venue locations for couples. A local venue had taken couples' deposits and then closed the venue doors. Geo had acquired a list from someone who had access to all the couples who needed to find new venues. A mishap of a venue shutting its doors is one of the worst tragedies in the wedding industry, not only for couples but also as a poor reflection on the industry. I honestly couldn't believe she wanted to unselfishly assist the couples. There was something about all these interconnected circumstances that made me say yes to joining the crusade.

That yes, and her ask, turned into a whirlwind of changes, personal growth, a bigger picture, a pandemic, a bond, and a business.

Then the pandemic occurred, venues and wedding vendors began shutting down their businesses and closing their doors. Here came an enormously magnified issue, as we encountered before when helping couples process the closing of one venue, and now there was a whole city's worth. The wedding industry and the couples unable to get married became a battleground. Instead of jumping into the boxing ring of verbal bashings and bad reviews, we worked to solve the problems for which none of us were responsible. Geo opened her wedding venue, and I used my planning company as the backdrop for weddings when Texas only allowed ten guests per wedding. Amid the world shutting down, we invited couples to get married safely, cleanly, and quickly. We promptly pivoted, changed our contracts, made people sign waivers, cleaned everything ferociously, wore irritating masks, and gave away approximately $55,000 in wedding services. We helped our faithful vendors keep their businesses afloat. We also began a podcast aimed at keeping couples and the wedding industry discussing solutions instead of arguing over deposits and dates.

Rapid transformation and expansion, both professionally and personally, resulted from that unstable time frame. We vigorously planned many weddings, creatively changed up timelines, and honed in on the essential wedding details to create magical moments. Our businesses began to expand and bloom. So why, in the pinnacle of paving a way, a rise in revenue, and building our brands, did we come to the pause on the swings?

We were two strong-willed, assertive, hardworking women on a set course, yet neither of us yearned to continue. We both were exhausted, and this exhaustion passed the hot, humid Houston heat. We had come to a fork in the road, and it took one question to open up the possibilities of a reset.

A reset can be enticing and transformative. It allows you to go back to the beginning, to redo or start again from where you began. Going back meant negating the changes and growth occurring to us separately yet simultaneously. We didn't want to go back to origination but rather to restart at this present time in our journey.

Geovanna, affectionately known as Geo once you meet her, was born in Mexico City and moved to Houston, Texas, with her parents by age five. Moving from Mexico to the United States is a beautifully familiar story we hear living near the southern borders and in one of the largest metropolitan cities in America. However, Geo's journey ignites a spark that powerfully reflects Latina DNA.

Geo was an energetic young girl who excelled in soccer enough to be sought after for a scholarship to attend college. This reflective feat proved her hard work and years of dedication had paid off. However, even at a young age, Geo began seeking a path that would go contrary to her parents' wishes for her future. Geovanna declined the college scholarship and started her corporate career, scaling the ladder quickly. The popular pursuit of financial affluence brought financial advantages, two beautiful children, her first marriage, and corporate success. There were ups and downs, like many young women juggling balancing a corporate community and a family lifestyle. Her life decisions were often met with cross-eyes, frowns, and questions from those around her as she pursued to advance her career. We all experience peer pressure to go with the flow, stay in the comfortable lane, and not rock the social norms that get you kicked off the boat. Geo's strong sense of identity has guided her to stick to her vision of a life she wanted to create, regardless of being coerced to walk the plank.

Geovanna is a force of nature, a beacon of light in the often competitive and cutthroat world. As a force of nature, she knew she needed to be on a path of creating the life she wanted, but this required more choices to go against advice and norms. Often, advice can be accurate and give insight if someone feels misguided or has swerved from their life's path. But, when you have a deep self-intention, you avoid the popular path; you respect the advice, yet not with much attention. Not because we are wayward people, as we may be perceived, but because there is this call, a pull, and a natural lean to forge a different path. Scouring, digging, and discovering become the light that guides us.

Sometimes, the path is smooth, and sometimes paved with potholes; believe me, we live in Houston, the reigning city of potholes. Regardless of how often we need to reset or be aligned, the rugged terrain does not deter us from trying new roads. Geovanna is just that woman. She remarried and found the perfect counterbalance to support and encourage her sense of ingenuity. Even their five-year courtship to marriage speaks to her unwavering desire to put herself and her children first. Again, it is a social norm that sounds great and triumphant while reading a book but is too scary and aggressive to pursue for most. We watch and learn from those who excel at driving on unpaved roads. We don't copy their actions but edify the determination to pursue what they see as theirs to achieve. Reflecting on who they are, their strength, character, resilience, confidence, and sense of identity gives us the hope and drive to tread our paths outside well-worn treads.

It's in the reflection of another and the light they shine that we reflect our light, no matter how dim or bright. Geovanna's magnetic personality draws people to her like moths to a flame, her infectious laughter and genuine smile leaving an indelible mark on everyone she meets. She is a true gem, a shining example of leadership, generosity, and creativity.

I often visualize our universes uniting as they did on a linear train track. Geovanna is at the end of the track, and I am on the opposite side, magnetically drawn to each other. We were traveling rapidly, hustling, and experiencing life simultaneously, on the same path but in opposite directions. When you meet us, our differences are apparent: we are 13 years apart, from 2 different generations, with a 6-inch difference in height, with varied body structures, voices, humor, and personalities. The list is endless. How did we get to where we are and make it?

My Latina heritage reminds me of a beautifully crafted kaleidoscope. Like the kaleidoscope, each one of us has unique patterns and characteristics. These patterns change in different lights or environments and reveal our authentic selves. I am a Latina with the genetics of a Latina, yet I was raised in a mid-American community with mostly Anglos, a term I heard my parents use. My experiences being a Mexican American unveiled on birthdays with homemade tacos, piñatas, and cajeta heavily poured on vanilla ice cream (no pun intended). On Saturday mornings, my dad would spend hours in our garage after a long week as an expert lubricant engineer. He built furniture, carved wood, and took on house and garden projects for our family and neighbors. He worked and whittled while listening to José Alfredo Jiménez and Vicente Fernández.

We lived in Oregon, and my extended family resided in El Paso, Texas, or nearby. It was only on family vacations that I was around my extended family, listening to my grandfather's old stories, seeing my grandmother cook endlessly in the kitchen, making her legendary dishes, and crossing the border to Juárez, Mexico. All my cousins speak Spanish; although my parents did, my siblings and I did not. Of course, everyone was loving, but even as a little girl, I knew we were considered different. It's a unique place to be when you don't really 'fit' in one place or the other. The idea of not being 'Mexican enough' to some people and 'too Mexican' to others, each having their own expressed opinion based on their own life experiences. My parents were very welcoming, and we often had a house full of family and friends. I didn't feel isolated; on the contrary, I believe it helped me see everyone from the inside out instead of the outside in.

After college, I married a Christian pastor and had four immensely wonderful children. My children are half Mexican and half Creole-African American, and we came up with our own identifying race term, *Blacksican*. In those early years, there was a larger story that led to a divorce, by my choice, and the journey of a single mom of four. I began seeking my existence and identity during college, and the intrigue of my Catholic upbringing intertwined. I firmly believed in my parents' faith, just like their parents had taught them for generations. The encounter of learning more from nondenominational Christians heightened my desire to learn more and be devoted to God, hence marrying a pastor. Along those pivotal points of life, I lost who I was and created to be.

When I share my story in greater detail, I often get asked the 'how.' How did I lose myself when seemingly devoted to God and my family? I quickly gave the general, memorized, and noncontroversial response. At my core, I wanted to be accepted, forgiven, and ultimately loved, which I know God did, but unfortunately, man-made religion sometimes does not offer that same love. God's unconditional love became overpowered by conditions, rules, regulations, and standards, and when you sincerely want to be accepted, sometimes you lose yourself, even when it's others' misinterpretations of manuscripts. I take full responsibility now, but it was unhealthy teachings and my loss of self that opened up a contaminated mix to fester for years.

Even after my divorce, I tried resetting myself to move past the hurt but wasn't very successful. I was still stuck in old patterns of behavior, seeking love in the wrong places and barely getting by as a single mom. I did not prioritize my time and make myself a priority. I went through more years of living the mundane life of societal expectations, and sometimes disappointments for not living up to others' expectations. It was a vicious cycle repeating itself over and over.

Being mentally strong and able to place things in cerebral compartments was how I survived for so long. I was exhausted both mentally and physically, always trying to keep up and draining myself with those unhealthy patterns. Before the pandemic, I just got sick of myself. I don't know if others ever feel like that, but sometimes you just think enough is enough and repeat to yourself, 'damn, can we just stop?' The internal disgust began the changes. I was on a quest to regroup and figure myself out! I started reading books, doing deep-dive searches on Google, and looking for a sense of God in new yet profound ways.

This time, my quest was different. My senses returned, my love for people reemerged, and my passion for myself slowly began to take root. So, what was the difference this time? I shed the layers of the past, looked in the mirror, and accepted the things I could not change, devoting my energy to change the things I could. I began to find joy in creating my dreams and welcomed the availability to discover, all over again, my desires and passions. This time through my lens of the universal God that made me.

On a hot and humid day in August, my sense of explosion within me was at a peak. I had had enough, and the changes inside me had grown strong enough to ask Geovanna aloud that same question: "What are we doing?"

That one question sparked our reset, but this time in an incomprehensible way. Two women are going through life on the same train track yet in different directions, intersecting in a moment that leads to a brand and business. We knew if we were going through these changes, emotions, and desire to create more, other women were too. All the how-tos began to creep in, and the doubting people around us gave their opinions of how hard it is to start a new business.

"Why would you start over when you are doing so well?"

"How do you know you can trust this person?"

"How will you make it financially?"

We still get negative feedback from critics and naysayers.

Yes, we are determined; we did the work and will continue to do so. We work to turn shortcomings into advantages and expand our strengths, gifts, and talents into the foundation of our brand and business. Our zones of genius have been identified and developed. We have amplified our voices to help other women master their relationship with SELF, which is the key to prosperity in life, relationships, love, and business.

If turning down a soccer scholarship, enduring religious ridicule, and leaping off metaphorical cliffs means we will discover more for ourselves and others, then we say YES! Our sacred Latina heritage anchors our resilience and determination. This heritage, rich with the perseverance of the women who blazed trails before us, fuels our progress and the advancement of women's rights. Our daughters, nieces, cousins, sisters, and friends are empowered by their Latina DNA and driven by passion to build collaborations, brands, and businesses. We are all 'Latinas Rising,' inheritors of a uniquely crafted legacy. No matter the direction your journey takes, keep moving forward, creating your beautiful kaleidoscope!

ABOUT YG COLLABORATIONS

Ready to meet your inner powerhouse? Yvette Valdenegro and Geovanna Burgess White are the dynamic duo behind YG Collaborations! Though 13 years apart and stylistically opposite, their bond is magical and eternal. Amid the COVID-19 crisis, they defied industry shutdowns by keeping weddings alive through strategic collaborations, discovering their mission to help women unmask their genius and break societal barriers.

The vision behind YG Collaborations is to fortify women's relationships with themselves. With most businesses failing within five years due to self, time, and money issues, Yvette and Geovanna's coaching targets these crucial areas. Their leadership on boards and groups embodies their advocacy for women at every step. Blending creativity, intuition, and unwavering strength, their coaching helps clients exceed their own expectations. Through YG Collaborations, they disrupt norms and spearhead Houston's exclusive YGC Collective, a conference crafted by women, for women, of all backgrounds.

Website: www.ygcollaborations.com
Instagram: www.instagram.com/ygcollaborations
Email: hello@YGCollaborations.com

ABOUT AMA PUBLISHING

AMA Publishing is an international, award winning publishing company that champions the stories of entrepreneurs who are trailblazers, innovators, and instigators.

Forbes has said that, *"AMA Publishing is helping women reshape the future of publishing."*

We would love to help you tell your story. We have helped thousands of people become international, bestselling authors through our courses, multi-author books, and as solo authors.

Your story, it's ready to be told.

Website: www.amapublishing.co

Made in the USA
Las Vegas, NV
01 October 2024